there's anything
can do…

If there's anything I can do…

How to help someone who
has been bereaved

Caroline Doughty

Editor: Roni Jay

WHiTe LaDDEr PRESS

new tricks for old dogs

Published by White Ladder Press Ltd

Great Ambrook, Near Ipplepen, Devon TQ12 5UL

01803 813343

www.whiteladderpress.com

First published in Great Britain in 2007

10 9 8 7 6 5 4 3 2 1

13-digit isbn 978 1 905410 19 4

British Library Cataloguing in Publication Data

A CIP record for this book can be obtained from the British Library.

Designed and typeset by Julie Martin Ltd
Cover design by Julie Martin Ltd
Printed and bound by TJ International Ltd, Padstow, Cornwall
Cover printed by St Austell Printing Company
Printed on totally chlorine-free paper
The paper used for the text pages of this book is FSC certified.
FSC (The Forest Stewardship Council) is an international
network to promote responsible management of the world's forests.

FSC
Mixed Sources
Product group from well-managed
forests and other controlled sources

Cert no. SGS-COC-2482
www.fsc.org
© 1996 Forest Stewardship Council

 White Ladder books are distributed in the UK by Virgin Books

White Ladder Press
Great Ambrook, Near Ipplepen, Devon TQ12 5UL
01803 813343
www.whiteladderpress.com

To Nick

Thanks

This book could not have been written without the help and contributions of many people who were willing to give me an insight into their own experience of widowhood.

Together we have experienced a wealth of love, support, kindness, friendship and understanding. By combining examples of brilliant ways in which our friends and families have helped us, and the things we would have appreciated, we hope we can give ideas to others who want to help a grieving friend.

All the people who contributed to this book have lived through one of life's biggest challenges and I thank them all for sharing their experiences with me and allowing me to quote them:

Kajsa Aslin, Fiona Bailey, Celia Barker, Martin Brass, Lynn Bendle, Lucy Brazg, Annette Chellingsworth, David Chivers, Zoe Cooper, Rosemary Cruikshank, Judith Cunnison, Marion Dawson, Melanie Dawson, Beth Diskin-Kremer, Jean Dixon, Jim Drummond, Mary Dunn, Eric Edwards, Alison Green, Rachel Green, Michael Hunt, Roni Jay, Jane Keightley, Patsy Kemp, Kim Mason, Angus MacKinnon, Gill Morgan, Emma Marriott, Alistair Morris, Wendy Morris, Andrew Parkinson, Maddy Paxman, Lisa Pegg, Laura Roberts, Vanessa Rumball, Julie Southern, Kay Spriggs, Lisa Stewart, Irene Stratton, Robin Walker, Gordon Wilson, Paul Wright.

I would also like to thank The WAY Foundation.

WAY was set up 10 years ago to provide a support network to people widowed under 50. It is now a national organisation with local groups throughout Britain. I have made friendships through WAY that I hope will last a lifetime, with people who really do understand what it is like to lose a partner, soulmate and best friend. We've shared a lot of memories, laughter, tears and bottles of wine over the years and many WAY members have helped with this book. You can find out more about The WAY Foundation at **www.wayfoundation.org.uk**

I would also like to thank those who have supported me over the last five years. I have always known I am surrounded by love, and that has kept me going.

With my deepest thanks to Ellie and Laura for giving me a future, I love you more than I can say; to Mum and Dad for your constant love and help; Dilys and Tony for your unwavering support and love; Pip, Jonathan, Matthew and Debbie for making me part of your family and helping raise Nick's girls with so much love; Steph and Sam for such support and love despite the distance; Sally and David, for your unwavering love, encouragement and endless hours of childcare – I couldn't have done it without you; Denise for the love, laughter and crazy holidays; Emma for the marathon, a lifetime's friendship and moral support; Lee for always being here with love and encouragement; Keith for advice, friendship and being there with Nick; Kevin, Erik, Tom, Camilla, Una and Arlene for so many happy memories; Sam and Ian for great friendship and France; Jules and Paul for Greece and the inspiration to write this book; Beth for your friendship, understanding and love; Zoe for Sunday afternoon camaraderie; Ruth, Kim, Kajsa, Simon, Anne-Marie, Alistair, Jenny, Helen, Debbie, Martin, Rachel, Maddy, Helen, Martin and all my other WAY friends for your incredible support, understanding and great company; Paula, Steve, Ben, Phil, Peggy, Dan, Caitriona for being our shared friends and still being there; James for doing my job, reminding me what fun is and being a true friend; John and Jara for being there in moments of crisis and for still talking about Nick; all my other friends who have made me laugh and kept me company; Father Andrew and Mother Clare for helping us all through the most difficult days; Rosemary for your support and help; Jennifer, Maria and Leticia; Rebecca for caring for the girls and making them happy when I didn't have the strength; Jill for your help with this book and loyalty to everything Nick wrote – sorry we never quite got there; Elizabeth for keeping me sane; the Macmillan team at the Royal Free Hospital; Zarine for your unquestioning support from day one; everyone at Justgiving for making me feel normal and finally Roni for supporting this project and sticking with it despite your own tragedy. Richard would be so proud of you all and I'm sorry he won't see this in print – although I'm sure he'd see the irony of choosing to publish it.

Contents

Preface

In early 2002 our lives seemed too good to be true. Our second daughter Laura had been born healthy, bouncy and bright; our toddler Ellie was a delight and Nick's writing was going well. Life couldn't have been better and we felt truly happy.

But Nick began to feel unwell. He was tired and had odd pains in his back. After many visits to the GP and various tests he was getting no better and took himself to A&E. They admitted him and a week later he was diagnosed as having stage four cancer of the oesophagus. We knew from the beginning that Nick's cancer would kill him – his doctors gave him two and a half years at most.

Our world was shattered and I knew then that whatever happened, and however long he was able to fight the disease, I would be a young widow.

Nick responded well to his treatment at first and we both tried hard to believe he would live much longer than predicted. "Apart from being riddled with cancer I'm a fit, healthy guy," he would joke. We talked about how the statistics included men in their seventies and eighties and how he *had* to be at the top end of the range, given the fact he was only 41.

But as we moved into 2003 the treatment was having less effect and on Good Friday we were told there was nothing more the doctors could do. Nick died nine weeks later on June 23, at home, surrounded by his family.

The following weeks are a bit of a blur – I have very little memory of anything that happened except for brief snapshots of the funeral, the party afterwards – a riotous affair that Nick would have loved – and a holiday we shared with some old friends of his in their summerhouse in Denmark. It was a quiet, simple wooden house on a Danish beach, with dunes covered in wild flowers, where the children ran around happily with their friends and played in the sea. The relief that Nick's illness had finally ended breathed life into us and it was good to walk, swim, laugh and be with friends. After a year of living under the shadow of cancer my worst nightmare had come true, the day I'd been dreading since the moment of diagnosis had come and gone, and nothing could ever be that bad again. Despite our desperate sadness and grief, it was, in a bizarre way, liberating.

But as the reality of being a young widow with two small children set in, those initial feelings of relief disappeared and were replaced with a tortuous grief that tore at me from the inside until it slowly subsided to be replaced with a lingering, heavy sadness that has certainly lightened with time but will never entirely leave.

The writer and Agony Aunt Katharine Whitehorn who was widowed after 45 years of marriage said: "It's when the drama is over and you face the grey mudflats of the future that the real widowhood begins… You don't 'get over' the man, though you do after a year or two get over the death; but you have to learn to live in another country in which you're an unwilling refugee."

Friends rally round at the beginning, they are grieving too and there's a remarkable closeness as you cry and laugh together, remembering the old times and talking about the person who is no longer at the table.

But now, four years after Nick died, I inhabit a very different place.

I still feel that I don't belong – I am not married, yet often I don't feel single; I am a single parent but feel less than half of what I was in a couple. There is no one to share this overwhelming task with and the comfort, support and sustenance I got from being part of a couple has gone. What is left is one person, but a person who is in some ways less than she was; I am too young to look like a widow, people are shocked when I tell them. I still steel myself for the reaction when the question is asked and it gets easier over time, but always reinforces the fact that my situation is not ordinary.

For those thrown into widowhood in their fifties or sixties the feelings are different but nonetheless overwhelming. Children, if there were any, have left home and now there is a deafening silence where once there was conversation. No one will put a key in the lock, there is no one to discuss the day's events with. Children are busy with their own lives and the future you'd planned to have together once they'd left home has disappeared. It may look empty and bleak and for those widowed at this age there is a long life left ahead of them – they are not 'old'.

Nick used to say that becoming a parent was like crossing a one-way bridge into a new land. It changes you as a person and you can never go back. Losing a partner takes you over another of life's one-way bridges. It changes your perception of the world. It robs you of an innocence you weren't aware you had. It means you will never be able to think 'It won't happen to us'. It did, and it was as bad as it can get. Yet bizarrely there are positives. Losing a partner makes you value so much more about life – it puts things in perspective, makes you realise what's important. I've met many widows and widowers who've changed their lives radically – moved homes, got new jobs, stopped working, reinvented themselves, travelled the world, had children. We inhabit a place where you really know that you can go to bed one night and not wake up in the morning. The five year plan to pay off the mortgage, or save up for a new car or holiday seems like nonsense. We know that the simple things matter in life – and that they matter today.

As my relatives are all fairly far-flung their support has been concentrated into school holidays, weekends, flying visits and phone calls. I don't think I would still be sane had it not been for them, and for the friends who have supported me week in, week out, through some very difficult times and who have had to listen to hours of grief, anger, incomprehension, bitterness and sadness.

Friends have looked after the girls endlessly, cooked us food, stayed the night, got drunk with me, helped me begin to stagger through the minefield of dating and some of them, incredibly, are still laughing. I love each of them more than I can say and it is as a tribute to them, and the family that loves me and the girls so much, that I decided to write this book.

But there have been times as I've travelled this long, lonely road, when people haven't known what to say or do and when even the closest of friendships have strained at the seams; when I walked back into work and a silence fell across the office as people looked down at their desks, unaware of how to treat me; when mothers from my girls' nursery dodged into another aisle in Sainsbury's to avoid having to face me; when I realised that friends had stopped calling or visiting because listening to my unending pain was just becoming too much.

Death is the last taboo in our culture – we can talk about anything else but that. When it involves the young it is even worse. People are scared of death and of the great engulfing emotions it brings in its wake. Married couples, especially older couples, think: 'There but for the grace of God' and shy away – they fear that death could be catching – it might be them next and they don't want to have to face that reality.

The grief of a friend can be a terrible thing to witness. There is nothing you can do to stem the tide, and yet, you really do want to help.

One thing I have learned since Nick's death is that the road is longer and harder than I could have imagined. Grief is with you, every day, like a load on your back. It gets lighter over time but it may never disappear completely. Sometimes you realise it's gone, and the periods without it grow longer and become more frequent, but it still returns and brings you crashing down at unexpected moments and for unpredictable periods of time – maybe an hour, a day or two, maybe a few weeks.

Widows and widowers who have remarried say they still grieve for husbands and wives who died many years before. Even falling in love again doesn't wipe the slate clean and it's irrelevant whether they had children or not – widowed people will still grieve for the future they will never have. For those with children, whether they are now three or 33, there will be a sadness that the person they made those children with is no longer around to share in their lives, achievements and successes. Birthdays, first school days, graduations, weddings, grandchildren make the bereaved parent feel again the weight of loss of the partner who has died. It is important that friends and family are aware that this can go on for many, many years, even if it is not discussed. Life events will always be tinged with sadness and even years later, grief can catch you unexpectedly and take your breath away with its strength.

I wrote this book as a way of saying thank you to the numerous friends and relatives who have helped me on my journey back to some kind of normality, and as an inspiration to the friends, family, colleagues and neighbours of others who will one day be grieving for a much loved partner.

You can help. You can ease the pain. You can never bring back the person who has died, which is all your friend really wants. But there are dozens of things you can do to lighten the load he or she has to carry. And you can keep on doing it, not for a few weeks but for months and years. If anything, it is even more important later on than in the first hazy weeks when their world has quite simply been torn apart. It takes a long time to repair that sort of damage and it is over those long months and years that they will need your love, support and company.

It doesn't need to feel like an onerous task – many of the ideas in this book are simple, easy things that are part and parcel of friendship, but can still make a big difference to someone who is grieving.

I have written this book from the perspective of someone whose partner, husband or wife has died, which is my own experience. Yet much of what is written here will be appropriate to someone grieving for the loss of a child, sister, brother, close friend or parent.

CHAPTER ONE

The listening ear

When Nick died we lived in London. We had a terraced house on a lovely quiet street with great neighbours. I had local friends, mostly made through the girls' nursery, and a couple of friends from my ante-natal class. My parents were in Edinburgh, where I'd grown up. My sister was in Scotland at the time but moved to New Zealand eight months later. Nick's parents were 100 miles away, his sister and brother both outside London. None were near enough for last minute babysitting or emergency hugs so it was down to my friends to keep me going on a day to day basis.

They have been truly amazing over the last few years. Between them they have made me laugh, cry and helped me reach the bottom of many bottles of wine. One neighbour appeared instantly several times when I phoned in a panic, another regularly helped look after one or both of the girls. Parents of my children's friends have done way more than their fair share of fetching, carrying and looking after, and to them I will be eternally grateful.

When someone dies, their death doesn't only affect the immediate family. It can have an unsettling effect on the lives and relationships of friends, colleagues and neighbours too. A death is like a pebble being thrown into water – creating a dramatic splash and then being followed by ripples that continue to spread outwards.

Looking back on the last few years, one of the things that has most surprised me is the way Nick's death affected so many of my friendships. I didn't realise it would happen and the result has been, at times, quite hard for many of us to cope with.

Many friendships have deepened and wonderful new relationships have grown. Others have been tested by years of grief and a few have simply died, as friendships do over time under any circumstances.

The friends of someone who is bereaved fall into different categories:

- There are the new friends who didn't know your partner. They are great for helping you move on with your life, discovering new interests, making new attachments and growing as a person.

- There are the couples you used to socialise with together. Being with them can be comforting and reassuring, but can also be hard as you watch two people live and grow together in a way you never will.

- Then there are the married friends who aren't getting on very well, which is hard because you just want to shake them and say 'can't you realise how lucky you are to have each other?' – not always appropriate and not the best way to behave.

- There are divorced friends who have experienced many of the same feelings of loss so can be very empathetic, but who don't understand what it feels like to lose a partner when you both still loved each other.

- Then there are single friends who can be great company though a widowed person may not see themselves as single, but rather still married to someone who isn't there any more.

Watching a friend grieve for the loss of a much loved partner is a tall order. It's exhausting, relentless, difficult and at times boring to listen to the same things over and over. Your friend will require much patience and understanding, and the support you offer soon after the death will be different to the support they need later on.

This chapter deals with how you can support your friend in the immediate aftermath of their partner dying, and the weeks that follow.

There are many things you can do to help, whether you are local or live far away.

- Talk about their partner, and carry on doing so. Don't think you'll upset them – they are already more upset than you could imagine. Talking about the bereaved person makes it clear that they may have died but they haven't been forgotten, it is a way of recognising that you knew that person and it shows the bereaved that you still remember and think about their partner.

- Call and tell them you've been thinking about their husband or wife, recount a dream or a memory you've experienced. We all like talking about our friends and family when they're alive – well it's still the same when they're dead, if not more so.

- Phone regularly and keep it up for as long as you can after the death. By staying in very close contact you will be more aware of your friend's ups and downs. You'll know when they're struggling and likewise you'll hear when they're doing better and you can recognise that progress and encourage them. By phoning once every few months you may get a very skewed view of how they're really coping.

- Keep your calls short and phone when you know it's a good time. If you don't know when is a good time, then ask. Maybe your friend can't sleep and is awake late into the night and would appreciate someone to talk to. Maybe they're up at 5am with insomnia. Maybe when her husband would have normally come in from playing golf or football. When the kids have just gone to school and they come back to an empty house and the loneliness hits home extra hard. Or perhaps on a Sunday morning when they've got a long day ahead of them alone.

- A quick, regular call just to say you know they're there and you're thinking about them can make a big difference to a day.

- If your mother or father has recently been widowed, try and ring often, even if only for a few minutes. Older bereaved people will be nervous of being a burden on their grown-up children and may not contact them as often as they want to for fear of getting in the way or being a nuisance.

- Don't expect your widowed mother suddenly to want to babysit your children all the time. Yes, she may seem lonely, but she'd probably rather have your company than that of grandchildren who will require energy and stamina she doesn't have just now.

- If you see something your friend or parent might enjoy – an exhibition, a film, concert or sports match, suggest you go together. They won't want to go alone.

- Don't be offended if your friend doesn't reply to your calls – it can be hard work phoning people back and going over how things are, particularly if they're feeling low. Your friend might have the answerphone on, but they will still appreciate knowing you've rung up because you care.

- Don't try and get them to 'look on the bright side' or 'think positively'. Many bereaved people experience some form of depression – some more acutely than others – and they won't be able to see positive things that are happening at first.

- Keep an eye out for depression. If your friend is having trouble sleeping, is tired, irritable, low spirited, not eating properly then the chances are they are depressed and should seek some help. There is more information at the end of this book.

- Encourage your friend to talk to people who have been through a similar experience. Most hospices run support or friendship groups for relatives, there are organisations for people bereaved through suicide and road traffic accidents and several widowed people's organisations for younger and older widows. They will find people who have a clearer understanding of what they are going through and who they can socialise with. The White Ladder Press website has a full list of such groups (www.whiteladderpress.com).

- If a man is suddenly bringing up children alone, getting out to play sport, or go for a drink is going to be difficult. Once in a while ring up and suggest you have a beer at his house or watch a match there, rather than meeting in the pub and leaving him at home babysitting on his own. Not quite the same atmosphere but he'll appreciate the company. Better still, organise a babysitter for him so he can get out and join you.

- If you are in a couple, be aware that it might be hard for your friend to see you together, at least for a while. Think about seeing your friend separately as well, rather than always together, and when you are all together, acknowledge and talk about the person who has died.

- Do invite your friend to social occasions and try not to leave them out because they are no longer part of a couple. They might cancel at short notice if they don't have the courage to go at the last minute and this might happen more than once, but eventually they'll have the strength to join in again.

- Be careful how you arrange people around a dinner table – don't put the bereaved guest opposite the empty chair (yes, it really does happen!)

- If you are hosting a formal dinner make sure guests on either side of your friend know the circumstances. Being asked 'Where's your husband?' can be extremely difficult to answer in the early days of bereavement.

- Think about how you and other friends can help. Who is good at gardening? Who's a good cook? Who is free for a cup of tea in the afternoon once a week? Who could go for a walk once a week? Who does the same school run, or goes to football practice? Then ask those mutual friends if they'd do those things – it's easier for you to ask than the bereaved person.

- Collect memories of the deceased from other friends and write down your own memories in a book. Write to the children even if they are grown up – they'll appreciate reading about your relationship with their parent.

- Take over the decision making process temporarily – for an hour or two or a weekend. Come up with a plan and carry it out. If you're going out, decide where you're going to eat, book the table, arrange the transport, or choose a film and offer to buy the tickets. If you're staying in then arrange the food. Give your friend a break from having to make decisions all the time.

- Arrange a birthday party for your friend. It's a lonely process celebrating your first birthday after bereavement when there's no one around to make you feel special, give you a treat or tell you they love you. And if there are small children, make sure they have a present to give their mum or dad on their birthday, mother's or father's day and at Christmas.

- If your bereaved friend gives you something that belonged to their partner, don't pass it on to someone else – they've probably thought hard about who to give possessions to and why. If they give you something like jewellery, a watch, a pen or a bag then wear or use it occasionally to show your appreciation.

- Remember the birthday of their partner. You don't need to send flowers or a gift, but a card or a letter to show you've remembered is good. It's comforting for a bereaved person to know that other people haven't forgotten.

- Don't expect your friend to 'get over it'. They'll show fewer obvious signs of distress as time passes, but they'll never forget what's happened, even once they've learned to accept their new situation.

- Be aware that milestones and changes will affect your friend for a long time to come – other people becoming ill and/or dying, friends moving house, children leaving home or starting a new school, moving house themselves, leaving a job or starting a new one. Each of these transition periods are likely to stir up feelings of loss and change, and can bring back difficult emotions or make them feel panicky, even years later.

What people say about friendships

"Don't give advice, don't tell me how to grieve or that time is a great healer. I won't be able to hear you."

"I feel safe in the knowledge that any of my friends are only a phone call away and they are on my doorstep – probably with a bottle of wine and a box of tissues in hand anytime. I know this because a couple of times it's happened at 10 at night! I rang and they came – no questions asked. I'm not a needy person but sometimes your grief can scare even you with the manic thoughts that can go through your mind."

"I was getting very frustrated about people not mentioning Iestyn – this included family as well as friends – I had to say something as it was really upsetting me, as if they were trying to forget him and I had to tell them I didn't want to forget him and it was an insult to his memory."

"Good friends continue to talk about Jo, and have done since the start. It does frustrate me at times that many friends/acquaintances seem embarrassed to mention Jo in conversation, even after I may have done so."

"Please mention his name. Don't make the common mistake of thinking you didn't want to upset me. Do you really think I'm not upset anyway? Do you really think I'm not thinking about him 24 hours a day? One of the worst ways to upset me is making me think you have forgotten him. Grief is desperate, it's lonely, it's the worst thing. You can't make it any worse for me."

"I find it hurtful that none of the parents I've met through my sons' new school ever ask me about his Dad. It is as if he had never existed. They know my boys – are they not curious to know a bit about their father? Where he was from, what he did for a job, where we met – that kind of stuff. It's not like I have an ex-partner who I'd rather not talk about. This was my best friend, my lover, my husband and the father of my children and we talk about him every day at home. I'm proud of him and I'm sad people don't want to know about him. Maybe they're embarrassed, or don't know how to ask, or think they'll upset me – but when I mention him I wish they'd pick up that hint."

"I want people to phone and come round, and not think there's going to be a wailing woman on the phone. People have to be grown up about it – there are a lot of people in the same boat at my age. This is what happens. But people deliberately don't mention Robin, or the fact that he's died, and that's hard."

"I have been blessed with marvellous support from some people whom I would have never expected to have had such love and friendship and kindness from… It has taught me so much about human nature. It has also taught me not to make assumptions about people or relationships – I have learned such a lot about friends I thought I knew well."

"It's important for people to ring or write occasionally for years after, not just a few weeks. I simply didn't have the energy to respond, but I really appreciated their efforts."

"When times are grim, we feel unloved, neglected: regular contact – a knock on your door or a telephone call, can make a big difference. There doesn't have to be a particular reason for phoning, just seeing how things are."

"There were three sets of people – two couples and a business associate/friend who told me I could phone any time of day or night if I wanted to. I knew they meant it. I never needed them at 3am, but simply knowing I could phone did help enormously."

"The best friends have been the ones that phone and say they want to call in for a cup of tea. This gives me the social contact and friendship I need without any formality or the need to go out. I am working on going out more often and beginning to enjoy it more, but I still need help with it and the casual nature of just having a cup of tea and a chat helps me along."

"With grown-up children getting the level of communication is one of the hardest things. We always said we wouldn't be a burden to them, now I'm not sure when to ring, how much to ask of them. I wouldn't want to trouble them. To get lots of regular phone calls is good – they don't have to talk for long but the contact is the main thing."

"One of the things that hits you when your partner dies is the dreaded silence in the evenings, and having no one to share the observations of the day with. No one is really as interested in your family as you are, nor in your job and thoughts and feelings, so it is nice to have someone who phones regularly and shows a genuine interest in the things your partner would have been interested in."

"In the early stages, one or two really close friends didn't get in touch and I couldn't understand it, I was worried they hadn't understood the news or something… Later they confessed they didn't know what to say. My advice is – phone and say 'I am shocked to hear the dreadful news. I'm so sorry, I really don't know what to say.' That is so much better than saying nothing because you don't know what to say."

"Ken died in a diving accident and I only had one phone call from another member of the dive club. It turned out none of the others knew what to say, so they hadn't called. I felt as if when Ken died I'd disappeared too – because he was no longer there I didn't exist either. All they needed to say was that they were sorry he'd gone, an acknowledgment of what had happened. They didn't need to say anything clever, or to talk for long."

"When it comes to friends I had a few surprises. Some people are quite happy to talk about what has happened and chat about memories and some people tend to avoid it. And the funny thing is that the people I thought would avoid it tend to call more and make sure that we are OK and talk to me more than some of my friends that I thought I could count on 100%."

"I am really saddened by how few of my husband's friends ever call or visit. After the initial few weeks it was as if I and the children had just vanished. They remember the boys' birthdays, and we get a Christmas card or present, but they behave like distant relatives, not the great friends we used to laugh with, go on holiday with, share our lives with. I feel like they aren't interested in me or my children any more now that John's gone – like he was the one who was fun and interesting and they can't be bothered with me. In truth it's probably just a case of they've got busy lives and don't have time, and don't think about us that often. But I find it hard that they've disappeared from my life and I'm sad that the children don't have contact with them, which is what their Dad would have wanted. "

"I lost my wife, but I've also lost some very dear friends, and that really hurts."

"I try to limit the time I spend with married people who constantly talk about their partners – a lot of them do. If I think a social situation may be difficult, I don't do it, I avoid it if I can. I have come to realise that people who I was happy to go out with before may not be good for me now. I need to find new friends, but that requires confidence which is only now returning after two and a half years."

"I do find it hard to be with my regular friends. Either they don't have children, so their lifestyle and social life are not child friendly, which bars me from joining in most of the time. Or they are people with children in complete families and again, you feel isolated and an outsider. They are complete, they are whole. It rubs it in that you're on your own and it's very noticeable. Even six years later it's still the same."

"The guys never come over, they've never once suggested coming here instead of meeting in the pub. Michele's friends were rubbish as well. There's only one friend I stay in contact with. One thing I absolutely think is more important than anything else is the children. I can't believe they haven't stayed in touch with the kids for Michele, it's just completely bizarre."

"The worst for me was meeting up with our married friends who we had always done things as a foursome with in the past, who suddenly panicked and stopped phoning, or worse still tried to carry on as if nothing had happened. Some friends seemed completely oblivious to the fact that not only was I grieving for the loss of my husband, but also for the loss of my son's father. So to go on family days out with them seemed like a nice idea, but for me to hear 'Daddy get the bag, Daddy where are the sandwiches, it's your turn to change the nappy John, it's your turn to drive' etc just wore me down completely. They

thought we had all had a lovely day and they were doing their 'bit' – I would drive home in floods of tears, feeling devastated, emotionally drained and lonelier than ever before. Good things that friends can do – be conscious of the above, help me lift the buggy out of the car, carry my little boy on your shoulders or play football with him (the things his Daddy would be doing with him). Give my son some male attention, don't just ignore him and fuss around your own children all the time. My son has lost his only real male role model, imagine what it is like for him."

"Please, please, please do not try to compare grief with divorce and separation. Let me explain. A divorcee probably had some choice or influence in what happened, knows roughly where her husband is, might be in touch with him, can hear his voice and talk to him on the phone, can blame him, has someone to get angry with, still has a father for her children, has the possibility of reconciliation, is not grappling with the philosophical and metaphysical questions of the afterlife, and has not had to choose him a coffin…"

"Divorced friends I find the hardest of all, as they can talk insensitively about their exes in a rather derogatory light and all I want to do is shake them to say that I would do anything just to have my husband back. And wishing their exes dead, as one of my divorced friends has said, is horrendous."

"My husband's birthday came two months after his death and it was going to be a difficult day. I had two sons aged eight and 11 and would have stayed in and been miserable – I hated asking for help. It was a July day and mid-morning a lovely friend just turned up with her family and a huge picnic. She took us out to a National Trust park and we picnicked and had a good day. Had she asked me to do this I would have found excuses but sometimes when the choice is taken away – she just arrived with the picnic – it's easier."

"The nicest solution has been friends who have made a definite invitation with clear acceptance that I might cancel at virtually no notice – and when I did it didn't bother them a bit or put them off."

"I remember going out to dinner with two couples about three months or so after Juliet died. We sat down at the table, there were six chairs and you guessed it, I sat opposite the empty one – I felt crap as it really brought it home to me."

"If you've not lived through a traumatic situation you're likely to be irritated by people who can't make decisions, can't commit to dates etc. But most who have had a bereavement, serious accident etc will be much more understanding. The difficulty is that most of us under 50 haven't experienced much of what life can throw at us, so we're less tolerant and less understanding than we think."

"I think I would prefer to be asked than not asked and if it was a very large group, having someone to make the numbers even instead of odd might be nicer.

Single friends are easier because I don't feel I am taking them away from their partners or that they are being with me out of pity but would rather be with their partners. I feel all girls' nights out are easier now. But for the first few months all I could feel was jealousy that they were going home to husbands to relate their evening to and I had no one keeping my bed warm."

"My first mistake was to invite two couples for dinner and found five at the table upsetting. It was always good to be invited out but I preferred there to be even numbers at the table, with another woman on her own – it made me feel more comfortable."

"Sometimes I felt so embarrassed for the guest who had enquired after my husband that I was the one having to hold it together and change the subject for them, whilst trying not to burst into floods of tears myself."

"The first time I had friends for dinner after Ron died it was a fairly formal dinner in the dining room. I set the table as always, I made a lovely meal. I had everything organised and then I realised that Ron was not there. It broke my heart. Being the first time I had entertained they were close friends so we all cried together and after a few drinks we ate the meal and had a good evening. I vowed that I would never entertain like that again."

"To be honest, putting on a dinner party yourself, is the worst. I am obviously the odd one out. Being the menu planner, the shopper, the cook, the host and the washer upper at the end of a long evening and a bomb site of a kitchen is the pits. I felt like a skivvy and totally left out. It'll be a long time before I do that again."

"Lots of my friends have rallied round. They ask me out for lunch, or to go shopping or for a walk or to an exhibition. It's nice to spend time with people so I'm not sitting at home thinking about Peter, but sometimes the busy days are as hard as the empty ones. I come home, eager to tell Peter about something I've seen or something I've heard about a friend's grandchild and he's not there. There's no one to share the news with. And that's when the crushing loneliness of it all sets in and I feel simply dreadful. No one would believe how much I cry inside these four walls – I don't want to cry in public but at home sometimes I fear the tears will never stop, it's quite frightening."

"I hate anything to do with families… Everywhere you go it is always the mum, dad, child and then me and Henny by ourselves.

Anything from children's birthday parties, Sunday afternoons in the park, to Tesco on a Saturday. Or I might just be overreacting."

"A friend of ours put together a lovely book. It's quite different from collecting letters of condolence. It's very touching (though I can hardly bear to touch it even now!) as it gives little glimpses of what people saw in Sue. It's something that I'm sure the children will value enormously."

"People think that you're 'over it' after the first year or so. I wish they realised that the pain is always there and doesn't go away, and that life as a single parent is tough. I have recently started a new relationship, so people assume I'm 'over' Rob's death – I'm not!"

"I have never appreciated the wonder and simple joy of having a meal cooked for me as I do now. My best friend invited us over once at 6.30pm and I did nothing from the moment I walked in – food, wine, bedroom sorted, Alexandra bathed, bottled, storied, put to bed – I will never forget it."

"One of my good friends explained… They are scared of talking to us because it often makes them search their own inner feelings about being left alone – and let's face it no one wants to contemplate widowhood. That's why they want us to be OK and back to how we were before this tragedy hit us – what they can't ever realise is that we can't go back to how we were before. All of life's experiences change us and this is about as big as it gets. But what we can do is explain that talking about what has happened allows it to settle into a new perspective in our minds. From then on, when it ceases to be all consuming in our brain, we can start to develop a new path into the future."

GOLDEN RULES:

- Talk about the person who has died, don't be scared to use their name.

- Don't expect your friend to grieve in a certain way, or give advice about how they should be behaving or reacting.

- Work out what you are able to do, offer to do it and then do it – try not to cancel or let your friend down.

- Keep contact regular with short visits or a weekly phone call.

- Remember that being alone after decades of marriage is a daunting, even scary place and may continue to be so for some considerable time.

- Be aware of your friend's situation and try not to compare lone parenting or divorce to bereavement.

- Invite your friend out and keep doing so even if he cancels or declines several invitations. Eventually he will want to socialise again.

CHAPTER TWO

The trouble with comfort eating

I remember watching an episode of the TV series 'Cold Feet' when Nick was ill. Rachel had died in a car crash and her best friend Karen was in the supermarket. She looked at the Tunnock's caramel wafers on a shelf and promptly burst into tears, sobbing in the aisle as other shoppers looked on bemused.

It seemed contrived and sentimental to me. Surely a packet of biscuits couldn't reduce someone to tears... Yet only months later it was the fish counter that did it for me.

Nick was always a big fan of fish. One of my favourite photos of him was taken on a Croatian island where we sat in the sun at a table near the sea. We'd eaten fresh fish caught that day with tomato salad. Nick is pictured holding the fish bone up by the tail with a mischievous grin on his face – sunshine, the sea, and good, fresh fish to eat was his idea of heaven.

So there I was in Sainsbury's, slowing down by the fish counter thinking 'What shall I get for dinner tonight?' when slowly and painfully it dawned on me that I didn't really like fish that much, and I certainly didn't want to buy it and cook it for myself. Nick was gone, and there was no need to buy fish any more.

For Robin it was Marmite. For Susan it was broccoli.

It is one of the small but defining moments of widowhood; a mundane, regular activity that suddenly takes on a whole new significance. The fish business shouted at me loud and clear that Nick had gone and would not be coming back, my life was different now, I was no longer part of a couple and would now be cooking for one.

For most of us food is bound up with the important people in our lives. Eating is a social activity. We linger over breakfast together at home on Saturdays, we share our evening meal or eat lunch together with the kids at weekends.

After your partner dies it feels like that joy has gone forever. I remember a weekend in the early days when I sat down alone for seven meals with my children, from Friday tea to Sunday tea. By the last meal of the weekend I was too near to tears to talk. It had been a constant mantra of 'don't play with your food', 'eat up' and so on. No adult conversation, no jokes to one side, no discussion of what we would do later in the day or the next day, just me trying to sustain a conversation with a two year old and a four year old and hating the fact that I was on my own.

There are few things that bring the situation home more clearly than sitting alone at the table with your children day in, day out, after your partner has gone. We may have come a long way from the 1950s image of the nuclear family sitting round the table eating dinner together, but the empty chair certainly takes on a whole new significance after death.

"I still have not been able to eat at the table where Ron and I had our meals a deux each evening. I tried it several times in the beginning but ended up breaking my heart and meals were spoilt. I now sit in front of the TV. I really don't like it but I still have not been able to go back to the table," said Marion, who was widowed after nearly 40 years of marriage.

As far as shopping went, I had been lucky. Nick often did it as he worked from home and used it as an excuse to get away from his desk. We didn't always like the same food, but had got used to catering to each other's tastes.

After he died I didn't know what to eat. I was paralysed in the supermarket. Twice I came home with the oddest assortment of nappies, drinks and some fruit but nothing to make a meal with. I lost count of the number of times I gave my children fish fingers.

This is no surprise to anyone who has been bereaved. It is widely accepted that making decisions when you are bereaved is one of the most difficult things to do. Grief saps you of energy, it drains you and makes you unable to decide on the tiniest, most mundane of things. There were many days when I literally couldn't decide what to eat, so I just didn't eat.

A friend who has always loved to cook told me she just stood in front of the fridge dipping bread sticks or crisps into humous after she'd put the kids to bed, and that was dinner. Easier than cooking, less effort than deciding what to make.

When Nick was diagnosed with cancer he decided he was going to give his body his best shot at beating the disease, and one of the most important components of the fight was going to be diet.

In came the juicer, a 'Healing Foods' cookbook, then a vegan one. I remember one day getting ready to go shopping when Nick sat me down at the kitchen table and gave me his new vegan cookbook, asking me to make some things out of it for him. I nearly wept. I was so tired and drained of energy the last thing I wanted to do was learn new recipes from a strange cookbook.

But we both did, and for short periods we ate more healthily than ever before (though I certainly don't miss quinoa). Then he would revert to eating three tins of Ambrosia creamed rice pudding a day and little else, when his spirit and his appetite failed him and my energy for prompting him to eat was low.

Neighbours and friends were great during this time at bringing us goodies to eat – home made cakes and biscuits always went down a treat with both us and the children. And having a constant stream of visitors through the house meant that they really came in useful.

But another thing that's really helpful at such a time is to bring a good, wholesome meal round that will feed your friend and their family, or any unexpected guests, and give them good nourishment. It doesn't have to be fancy or organic, it doesn't have to be 'health food', but something hearty that your friend won't have the time or energy to make will be hugely appreciated. A casserole, shepherd's pie or some really good healthy soup, with a nice lump of cheese.

Sarah said people would bring meals round often when her husband was in hospital, but not after he died, though she would have loved it to continue for a while. Zoe said one of her friends brought food the day after her husband died suddenly and without warning. "I still remember that, it was so thoughtful and there was just no way I was able to think about food." A friend of Kim's cooked an evening meal for her every day for two months.

One of the kindest and most surprising things that happened to us during Nick's illness was to do with food and is something I will never forget.

It was a Tuesday evening and we were sitting downstairs with Nick's parents. The doorbell rang. I went to get it and there was a young Australian man on the step with a big box. "Delivery for Nick," he said with a grin and a drawl.

Intrigued, I brought the box in and we opened it up. Inside was a selection of organic fruit and vegetables but we had no idea where it had come from.

After a bit of sleuthing the next day, Nick found out that a group of his friends had clubbed together and opened an account at an organic vegetable delivery company. From then on we had fresh fruit and vegetables delivered to the house every week. Admittedly, there were times when I simply had no idea how to cook some of the obscure vegetables we'd been sent and had to dive for the cookery book for inspiration. We identified squashes and gourds from a very handy colour photo and learned more new dishes.

It was a kind and thoughtful gift from people who wanted to give Nick the best chance possible of fighting his cancer and coping with the punishment of chemotherapy – and an extremely generous one too.

So here are some ideas of what you can do to make the whole shopping, cooking, eating headache a little easier for your bereaved friend:

- Bring food. Don't think that this is an old-fashioned or daft idea – every bereaved person I've spoken to who had food brought round to them appreciated it. If they don't want to eat it right away, they can freeze it for another day.

- Take good food for the children – it's one thing for a widowed adult to survive on Jaffa Cakes and bananas for a month or two, but children need better nourishment.

- Cakes and biscuits are nice to have but don't always bake for your friend. They'll need to eat savoury food too and will probably have had their fill of sweet things – you'd be surprised how many people turn up with chocolate, cake or the like as a gift.

- Try and arrange to meet for lunch instead of coffee and make sure your friend eats something that will sustain them.

- Go with your friend and do the supermarket shop together. Have a coffee afterwards as a reward. Keep them company, help them to focus, suggest some things to buy that will be relatively easy to cook. Remember they probably can't make any decisions at the moment so guide them gently.

- Ring when you're going to the supermarket and ask if there's anything they would like or need – make a couple of suggestions to help.

- Help set your friend up for online delivery from Tesco, Sainsbury's or Waitrose if they haven't done it before. It'll enable them to shop without having to brave the supermarket and can be far more convenient for people who are frail, don't drive, can't lift heavy bags or have children.

Many older widows and widowers never get back into the routine of cooking a proper meal once their partner has died. There seems little point. This is where good friends and neighbours can encourage them to eat by joining in and making it social.

- Invite your friend or neighbour for lunch, invite them at the weekends. Sundays can be a difficult and long day when you're on your own. If you've lived near each other for years and never eaten together it doesn't matter – what better time to start inviting them in and showing you care.

- Offer to go round to your friend's house and cook dinner. Take the ingredients, cook the meal, serve it and then clear up afterwards. For him or her it will be like going to a restaurant but without the hassle or cost of having to dress, go out, face the world or find a babysitter.

- Sometimes going out can be stressful and difficult – having someone bring the restaurant to you makes a lovely change. This applies to anyone, not just people with children – treating someone in their own home means they can enjoy good food and company without having to brave the world outside, which may still be far too difficult for them.

- Order your friend food from COOK, or give vouchers. They deliver home cooked meals, in one, two or four portion sizes, ready to put in the freezer. It's not the most economical way to eat, but it will ensure your friend has something nutritious and easy when they are too tired to cook but still hungry. COOK also does children's and babies' food (www.cook-food.net).

- Make a regular date to eat with your friend so they know they'll have company on a certain day.

- Don't expect a bereaved friend to be able to cope with dinner parties – even if you do have other singles there. They will feel in a strange no-man's-land. Married but without their partner, yet not ready to feel single. Making conversation with strangers can be tough for newly bereaved people who dread 'the question' and may not know how they'll respond. Invite them so they know they're welcome, but don't be insulted if they cancel once, twice, three times. They'll get there in the end. Don't stop inviting, but don't push.

- Offer to feed children – mealtimes can often be a very stressful time for parents. Turn up at 4.30, cook the kids something, serve it up, make it fun, get them to eat, then clear up the mess afterwards. Send your friend upstairs with a cup of tea, magazine and a cake – or a gin and tonic and a good book – whatever he or she fancies. Tell them not to reappear for an hour.

- If you can't cook or haven't a clue what sort of food children will eat, just be there at mealtimes. Sit with them, chat to the kids – just try and relieve the pressure of being a lonely, only parent for one meal at least.

- For older widowed people eating alone can be heart wrenching after sharing meals for 30 or 40 years. If your neighbour or friend is now living alone, be aware that he or she might not want to eat at all and that cooking could be hard for a long time to come. If there is not the necessity to cook for children then it can be even harder to make the effort for yourself.

How we feel about shopping, cooking and eating

"Two days after my wife died the fridge and freezer were completely full of food that people had brought round. Anne and Brian came over with more food and I didn't have room. Anne reminded Brian that they had an old freezer in the garage so he got up, went home and

came back with a freezer! We put it in my garage and within a week I had a six months' supply of food – it was absolutely brilliant. That's part of being male and Jewish I guess…"

"A very close friend and neighbour used to make a casserole or similar dish about once a week for the first month. She'd call in for a cup of tea and leave the dish by the cooker. She knew that I wasn't eating, but she never fussed. She'd just say, 'Don't forget to heat that in the oven before you eat it.' Her meals were the absolute best: nourishment, warmth and served with love."

"I was overwhelmed by the support neighbours gave me at the beginning. A Moroccan couple turning up with marinated chickens and all the veg. A French lady turning up with home made vegetable soup, an Irish lady turning up with home cooked bread. All this was good but was short lived – it petered out after a couple of months and no one made food again. I think people think that you start to recover a lot sooner than you do. I think the message I'd give to neighbours and friends is to keep coming back with meals and don't ask – just appear with it."

"To start with I used to go out for some milk and come home with washing up liquid. I'd go to the shop and have no idea what I was supposed to get when I was there. It might have been a good idea if someone could have offered to sort that out for me."

"Shopping is such an ordeal, as anyone in this position will know. I think it may have been helpful if someone had come shopping with me sometimes, because it had to be done, but could be impossible for me to manage. To be fair, I never asked anyone for this help and they probably didn't know how difficult I was finding it, or that for a while I gave up going out altogether and that was part of the reason I didn't always eat!"

"One family in particular has had us over for supper every

Thursday for the past year. It's like having relatives close by (which I don't), moreover I have come to realise that they really enjoy our visits and say that it makes their Thursdays seem special, which means I don't feel guilty for imposing."

"Henny and I ate pasta and sweetcorn for around two months after Barrie died. That was what she asked for and I was just on autopilot so I made it. Easy and quick to do and to be honest it didn't really bother me. I mentioned to my brother-in-law that we were having pasta and sweetcorn – he asked how often we had it and I told him every night. The next evening he came around with lots of food (he must have been up cooking all night and half the day), all packed up in containers to put in the freezer and just to take out, defrost and eat. He asked why I had not mentioned it earlier. I had never even thought about it."

"When I lived in the USA I was a member of a stay at home mom's group. One of its committees was set up to do just that – in the event of an emergency eg illness, job loss, death we would rally together a group and arrange for a week's worth of food to be made and delivered, fresh or frozen to the recipient's preference."

"Now I find cooking food such a bind. I love to try new recipes and my husband always said one of the things that made him rush faster home from work was the knowledge of something wonderful on the table awaiting him. Now if I try something new at least one of the kids, if not more, always finds fault and I never get thanks for my efforts."

"For the fortnight after Jo died a friend organised for cooked meals to be delivered each evening – made by three other friends on a rota basis."

"I have had one day off from cooking a week as my parents and in-

laws have come over once a week and done the main meal. This has been a great help in relieving the monotony of preparing, cooking and then clearing away."

"A few people in my village brought round casseroles or dishes for a few weeks after Michele died. They just did it, I didn't ask them. I'm always appreciative and grateful for people who help and I didn't feel at all insulted… Of course I would have liked it to continue! Most of our meals are fairly basic and simple – I miss having another adult at the table."

"I shopped on auto and after a while found I had a stockpile of Fruit and Fibre (shame the only person who ate the stuff had just died) and for some reason known to neither man nor beast a chicken mountain of skinless chicken fillets (approx 55 at one point believe it or not!) I also hit the manic healthy eating phase, as if by only eating whole grains and having five a day and all recommended daily allowances of vitamins and minerals would stop the children getting bowel cancer… It has taken nearly two years to calm down on this front."

GOLDEN RULES:

- Take your friend shopping or offer to shop for them.

- Cook meals – both during terminal illness and after bereavement.

- Invite them for lunch or dinner.

- Join in with kid's mealtimes to relieve pressure on a parent.

- Be aware that difficulties with food can continue for months if not years.

Shopping gets easier, but eating alone never gets more fun.

CHAPTER THREE

The loneliest job

Ellie was a week short of her fourth birthday when Nick died. Her sister Laura was 17 months old.

Although I had tried to prepare myself for what was to come I had no idea of what it would actually be like to raise two small children on my own. It was something I had never expected – Nick and I had married relatively late and our marriage was strong and happy.

Some 50 children and young people are bereaved of a parent in the UK every day, many of whom are babies or toddlers. Every month, hundreds of people have to begin raising their children alone, while coping with their own shattering grief at the same time.

Many people who contributed to this book talked about how they perceive being a widowed parent as different from ending up as a single parent through relationship breakdown, choosing to be a lone parent from the outset or bringing up children more or less single-handedly while a partner is travelling or working long hours. There are, without doubt, many similarities in the situations of all parents who are coping on their own.

However widows and widowers with children experience a unique loneliness. They watch their children grow, change and learn new skills yet with every achievement and success comes the sadness of knowing that the person they made those children with will never see any of it.

Even if children adapt to their new situation and grow up as happy, confident individuals and don't appear to be grieving for a dead parent, surviving parents still feel the weight of what their children have lost. They understand more than children possibly can about what that other parent would have meant to the family as a whole. They also have to come to terms with the fact that their partner is missing out on the amazing experience of watching his or her children grow up. As the WAY Foundation says, "When someone dies young, the grief of those left behind is twofold: the pain of losing the person they love and the pain of knowing what that person has lost."

The first time your children swim, pass exams or score a goal at football are moments that would make any parent's heart burst with pride. But for the widow, or widower, it also aches with sadness, for their child and for the other parent, knowing they will never again share these moments with each other.

Bereaved parents watch couples with their children sharing a joke, playing together, going out as a family, knowing they will never experience that with their child's other parent again. Preparing for a child's graduation, wedding or the arrival of a grandchild is always going to be bittersweet.

Bereavement is exhausting, relentless and often mixed with deep shock when the death was unexpected. The emotions it throws up are fierce and all consuming. And when you begin feeling better you can still be swept away at a moment's notice by the force of emotions that make you feel like you've been punched in the stomach.

Bereaved parents have to cope with this while at the same time learning how to do the hardest job in the world.

'You're doing so well,' 'You're so strong,' 'It's great to see you getting on with life,' are some of the comments bereaved parents hear often in the early days of grief. Quite probably they're not 'being strong' at all, but a child still needs breakfast every day, the school run still has to be done and shopping/washing/playing don't stop because a parent has died. As a bereaved parent you watch your partner die one day and the next day you get up at 6am or 7am and begin life as a single parent.

Parents rarely get the chance to do what every bereaved person needs to do regardless of age or situation – rest, sleep and slowly recuperate. What's more their children need extra support at a time when the parent is feeling fragile and scared, and they have to find their way through their own grief while trying to maintain a normal life for their children. Everyone knows coping with teenagers is tough – but doing it while you're all reeling with grief and emotions are stretched to breaking point is nearly impossible.

People say 'you should have a break, go away for a few days, get some rest' but your children need you close enough to touch all the time, day and night. They get scared when you go out that you won't come back, they need constant reassurance that you'll still be alive at the end of the school day or when they wake in the morning. If one parent has died suddenly and unexpectedly, what's to stop the other one doing the same thing? Now try and tell your child you're leaving for a week and they're going to their gran's…

A child's grief is something the parent has to watch, share and try to soothe, despite their own feelings of helplessness and emotional exhaustion. Younger children may grieve less obviously but their needs are tiring and demanding, while older children may require much more emotional input, needing to feel secure and loved at a time when they may feel angry, confused and deeply traumatised.

There is, of course, a huge consolation in being a widowed parent – children give you the best reason to get up every day, a reason to 'carry on' and to keep going. They are a constant reminder of the person who has died which can be comforting and prompt happy memories. Children still smile and laugh – and for them, grief is a different animal.

Winston's Wish, a charity founded to help grieving children and their families, describes it like this: "Adults could be said to wade with difficulty through rivers of grief, and may become stuck in the middle of a wide sea of grieving. For children, their grieving can seem more like leaping in and out of puddles."
See **www.winstonswish.org.uk** for more information.

Being a bereaved parent means you can rarely just curl up under the duvet, shut the world out and mourn your loss when you're so ragged and tired you feel you just can't cope any more.

There is also the responsibility. Suddenly widowed parents are solely responsible for making decisions about childcare and schooling, finances and work. They have to keep their children healthy and well fed, get them to school every day, care for them but discipline them too, stay up all night when they're sick, play with them despite being exhausted, cope with problems at school, exam stress, arguments with friends. They have to fetch and carry, sort out sports kits, make packed lunches and keep them entertained.

As well as the daily responsibilities there are the big decisions to be made alone, and while family and friends are often there as sounding board and interested party, parents can't expect others to help them decide about very important but personal matters such as childcare, schooling and guiding career choices. The tough thing is that these were decisions that would previously have been shared, debated and possibly argued over and now suddenly the bereaved parent is faced with having to come up with all the answers, maybe not knowing what their partner would have thought, or possibly trying to live up to expectations that are now much harder to meet. All at a time when just deciding what to eat seems impossible.

The phrase 'lone parent' has never seemed so apt.

So what can you, as a friend or relative, realistically do to make the situation seem less daunting and a bit more tolerable? How can you practically and usefully ease the grief?

- Try and give your friend as many breaks as possible. Don't turn up just after the kids have gone to bed (or worse, when she's trying to settle them down). Go round before tea time and give the kids their tea, then clear it up afterwards. Do it once a week – make it regular – and keep it up for more than just a few weeks.

- Try not to let your friend down – cancelling an offer to look after the children or take them out can be worse than not offering in the first place. Your friend will have been looking forward to the break more than you can imagine.

- When you arrive try and get your friend to sit down with a cup of tea, a beer, a glass of wine. Take control, tell them to disappear upstairs for an hour. And make it look as if you are in control, even if you're terrified.

- Help cajole teenagers into helping around the house and encourage them to do their bit with tidying their rooms, clearing up in the kitchen and so on. Your friend may not have the energy to nag or argue with older children but you can encourage them to help in a more enthusiastic way.

- Offer to help teenagers with homework, art projects and research – particularly if you have skills or knowledge of a particular area.

- Don't expect to be entertained – you're here to help, not be a guest. A confident friend who can take over, even temporarily, can give vital respite from the constant decision making required of a bereaved parent.

- Give small kids a bath – make it fun if they're not keen, splash around a bit, make them laugh. It's a great tonic for a parent to hear their kids laughing while someone else is looking after them.

- Ask if you can stay the night on a Friday or Saturday so you can get up in the morning with the kids – remember you can always have a nap later on, your friend probably won't be able to. Get the children up, give them breakfast and if you can, take them outside for an hour or two so their mum or dad can have a real lie-in. Oh, and a cup of tea and slice of toast in bed is the icing on the cake...

- Take over some of the weekend driving to football, rugby, music lessons etc. And remember that your friend will now find it difficult to go out late at night to pick up a teenager if there are younger children at home. Do as much of the fetching and carrying as you can – and don't expect to share it equally with them, this is your gift.

- Offer to babysit – for free. Watching their TV is as good as watching your own and it'll allow them to go out for a drink, see a friend or go to the cinema to escape for a while.

- Offer to babysit in the daytime too so your friend can go out and get some fresh air, have a walk, go to the gym, have a haircut, or do some shopping.

- Borrow an idea from a great neighbour of mine. Six months after Nick died, in the middle of winter, she started coming round at 8.30am twice a week so I could take Ellie to school without having to get Laura fed, dressed and take her too. Any mother of a two year old knows that letting them eat their toast slowly rather than fighting them into clothes to do a 10 minute school run has to be a better option! I'd go to school, have a peaceful five minute walk back home, a chat to my neighbour, then get Laura dressed in my own time. It was half an hour a day for my neighbour and it transformed the whole day for me, as well as giving me valuable time alone with Ellie.

- Share the school run, even if you have to go a little out of your way. Offer to do it once or twice a week, or make sure your friend knows that if ever they, or one of the children, is sick or unable to go out then you can step in and take one or other child to school. If you're a neighbour and you don't have children of your own, you're still fully qualified to do a school run and it'll be a whole new experience for you!

- Accompany your friend to parents' evening or be at home when they get back. Going to your first parent teacher meeting on your own is horrendous. It's typically the sort of thing you would go to together or if not, you would share with each other what the teacher had said afterwards. This time, you have to deal with everything that's said on your own and it's another vicious reminder that your partner will never be coming back. Parents' evenings can be especially tough when children are having problems at school following bereavement. Many children will find it hard to concentrate after the death of a parent and may be feeling angry or irritable. This can affect behaviour at school and interactions with peers. If staff are unaware of the situation, have forgotten or don't realise the effects bereavement can have on a child, explaining it can be harrowing, but doing it with a friend beside you will help. And when the news is good, having a sister, brother or friend around to congratulate you on what a great job you are doing as a parent goes a long way to ease the loneliness.

- If you are a Godfather or Godmother, think about doing a bit more than you might with other Godchildren – especially if you're the same sex as the person who has died. Remember your Godchildren have lost a crucial role model and will need other special adults in their lives. Don't just remember birthdays and Christmas, but think about being there when you can for things like school plays, assemblies and sports events. Take pride in your Godchild, be involved as he or she grows up. Phone and have a chat if you don't live near, use webcams, stay involved and make sure you get to know them. Be special – after all you were probably chosen by both parents for the role.

- Try not to compare your situation if you are often looking after your children on your own. 'I know how you feel, Jim's away at a conference so we can be widows together this week' is not a very helpful thing to say. If your partner is at work, even if they're away from home, you can talk on the phone or leave messages for each other and you know they'll be home at a certain time or on a given date. Even if you do the child-care every day, you probably have someone to moan at later on when they get home – it's simply not the same as knowing your partner will never walk through the door again.

- Offer to take children out, have them to play or sleep over. But avoid saying 'just let me know if you'd like me to have them'. It's always hard to ask someone to look after your children. It's especially hard when you're newly bereaved, at your lowest ebb and are possibly trying to cope without admitting you can't do it on your own. You don't know if the day is convenient for them, you know they might feel obliged to say yes when they don't really want to, and you don't know how long you can impose your kids on someone else for.

So friends – do it this way:

"I'd like to have them next Sunday. I'll pick them up at 11am, give them lunch, let them play for the afternoon, give them tea and bring them back at 6pm."

Why does this work?

Because your bereaved friend doesn't have to get dressed or leave the house, knows the date is convenient because you suggested it, knows exactly how long you're prepared to have the kids for and whether you're going to feed them. There will be no awkward mis-understandings and they will appreciate your offer more than you will know. I will never forget the friend who had that very conversation with me.

If you are a woman who has lost a female friend you can play a special role with her daughters, helping a bereaved father at a particularly difficult time.

- Offer to take the girls out shopping for new clothes, something they would have enjoyed doing with their mum.

- Have the girls back from school for tea once a week so they can build a relationship with you and know that there is a woman they can talk to if they need help or advice. Puberty can be a tricky time for girls and dads.

- Go out for a coffee with them – make them feel that you are a friend who enjoys their company and is willing to talk. If you have a dog suggest they come out for walks with you – people often find it easier to chat when they're outside and walking in the fresh air. They may not want to talk about their parent but they'll know that if they ever do they can come to you, and that's very valuable. Children often don't want to talk to a bereaved parent about how sad/angry/hurt they feel because they don't want to upset them.

- If your friend had sons then you can play a really important role as an adult woman who they feel safe with, have known for a long time – possibly all their lives – and can replace some of the 'mothering' that they have lost. Boys need this as much as girls.

For men it is important to keep up contact with your friend's children after his death. Sons particularly may not want to talk about their father's death, but they will appreciate having a male role model who they can trust.

- Take them out at weekends to play football, go fishing, watch a rugby match, go to a museum etc.

- Involve them in things you do with your own sons if you have them.

- Be active – their mum will be glad of a break and happy in the knowledge that someone else is tiring the boys out. Exercise is also a great way for older children to vent some of their feelings of frustration or anger in a safe way.

- Spend time with older boys so they know you're there for advice if needed.

For girls who've lost a father it's just as important to have a man around as much as possible – mine love the physical rough and tumble games they play with uncles and friends. Every time I watch them laugh and play like that, it makes me realise all over again what they have lost and how much they crave that attention.

It's crucially important to widowed parents that their partners' friends maintain a relationship with their children. They can tell stories about the parent who has died and are 'safe' for the children – they're not a new man or woman on the scene, coming into the house and destabilising children at a sensitive time. They're familiar people who children know and trust and as such their continued presence can provide valuable stability when a parent has died. If friends disappear it's another loss for the children as well as the bereaved parent.

How do bereaved parents feel?

"The hardest thing for me was asking. I was crying out for help but too scared, proud, exhausted, confused to ask for help. I'd always been a 'coper' and I didn't know how to admit that I felt like I was drowning."

"I managed to get the odd night away after my wife died but could have really done with going and sleeping at a different house – I just needed to sleep and wake up whenever without being woken up by kids… I would have much preferred people to be more pushy, but most of them sit back and wait to be asked – they don't know what to do."

"My overall experience has been that the most helpful people are those who get on and do something, rather than just offer vaguely, although maybe this is partly because I'm so bad at asking for help. I'm told that with English people you have to offer three times, because we all refuse at least twice out of politeness!"

"A number of people have offered to babysit to let me go out for an evening. This has been where neighbours are useful, or people with transport, as I can't fetch or return babysitters."

"Two male friends of Mike's have each had very regular contact with Ruairi, taking him to films or out for walks. As well as enjoying the time off this gives me, I like to feel that he has men in his life, who knew his father well. I feel sure that these two will be around long term for him as he grows into a man."

"My neighbour often looks after one or two of the children whilst I ferry others around to their activities, thus preventing the need to take everyone with me."

"Since Alison died I've been exhausted trying to cope with work, the kids and the house. My mate Paul does most of the taxi driving now for my teenage son who is best friends with his son. He'll go and fetch them at night and he does the footy run every Saturday. It gives me time to try and get on top of things and sometimes we all go together if I feel like getting out and having the company. But it's become a routine now and it makes such a difference."

"Richard had been a very active, involved father, so when one of my sons was invited on a camping weekend with his friend's family and the other was invited to go sailing, I felt this provided them with activities, fun and friendship in an environment I no longer felt able to provide. These were the best things people could do for us."

"A friend who is a mother of teenage girls has taken my girls clothes shopping. The friend has also had 'cooking/baking' sessions with the girls, often around Father's Day or Christmas and has used these to ensure the girls have brought me something… I am also a keen runner and to enable me to go running a friend has come round once a week to look after Elijah."

"One of my wife's friends has been amazing. Once every couple of weeks she leaves work early, comes over, hangs out with the girls and either helps them with projects for school, takes them for a bite to eat or just sits and chats to them about girls' stuff with a cup of tea. It's very low key, nothing special, but it's so great for them to be able to do that with a woman and they live for those evenings."

"I think the most useful thing that anybody can do is to offer childcare, or even just bring them home from school, football practice, parties etc. I know everybody says 'ask', but that is not always easy."

"Friends' offers to take the kids to 'fun' places were always a relief – not only for me to have a break, but to feel the kids were having a break from me at a time when I could not bear to have 'fun' time, even for them."

"I am so drained by the relentlessness of lone parenting that it would take more energy than I have to organise things that might make life better – like sleepovers for my son. I would really like people to just swoop in and take him off my hands without my having to plan it and ask for it."

"My friend's hubby just used to phone and say I'm coming for the boys, have them ready in 10 minutes. Then he'd arrive with their son, give me a huge hug and disappear off with the boys for a couple of hours – I can't even recall what I did with those hours but they allowed me to recharge my batteries and give my throat a rest from shouting at them. It stopped as soon as he could see I was coping but I know if I needed it again that Russ or Fiona would be there for me."

"One friend offered to have the boys every Wednesday of every school holiday for the foreseeable future. She knows that even though my grief will ease, the logistics of managing as a lone parent aren't going to go away, especially in the school holidays. It's good to know I can count on that help for as long as I need it."

"James started nursery for a couple of days and the first important date was the nativity play – he was a King… Going to the play was so hard, everyone around me was enjoying the occasion but I was just about holding it together – I wept buckets when I got home," said Paul. "James' first day at school and the girls' first day at nursery have been hard but other people don't seem to have a clue just how hard these days are – no one offered to go with me. If I had realised how hard the days would have been I would have asked but sometimes it just hits you when you are there."

"All milestones are a nightmare, along with birthdays and Father's Days."

"No one understands how difficult these days are unless they have been in the same situation. Last September, Keiron started school full time and it was also his 5th birthday. I was completely devastated that day at what his Dad was missing, and also what Kieron was missing, and cried taking him to school. I was still crying when I picked him up at 15.35."

'Mummy, please will you wave your magic wand and make Daddy come back?' were the most heartbreaking words I've ever heard."

Bereavement is utterly draining. One day you feel as if you're doing alright and coming out of a thick fog – the next you disappear right back into it again. Every contribution a friend or relative can make will help ease the day to day exhaustion provoked by the combination of grief and parenting. Even if your friend looks fine after a few weeks, it can take months for the swings of emotion to subside enough to be able to cope day in, day out without feeling total exhaustion.

GOLDEN RULES:

- Do little and often, rather than make one big sweeping gesture.

- Fetching and carrying can be an enormous help – do as much of it as you can.

- Take control for a little while.

- Show an interest in the children all year round, but don't forget special days and occasions.

- Don't wait to be asked. Think about what you can do and commit to doing it. Try not to let your friend down or cancel arrangements.

- Remember that you are important in the children's lives as a role model, so try and build a relationship with them.

CHAPTER FOUR

Getting out of admin hell

One of the hardest things a bereaved person has to deal with straight after a death is a seemingly endless mountain of paperwork.

Utility bills, council tax, phone, internet and other household accounts have to be switched into one name; joint bank and building society accounts have to be closed or names on them changed; pensions and benefits need to be claimed; insurance policies claimed or changed.

Some of this you can't do until you've got probate, which can take a year even when there is nothing complicated about the estate. And you can't begin any of it without a death certificate, which can take time to obtain if there was any uncertainty about the cause of death.

It can be very difficult to be clear headed and focused after bereavement. For months you feel like you are living life one day at a time. This is the advice you're given by books, counsellors and anyone with experience of bereavement – don't look too far forward, don't frighten yourself by thinking about a future alone, just focus on today, get through it, go to bed and then tomorrow focus on the day again.

It's a hard skill to learn, especially if you were someone who genuinely looked forward to the future and enjoyed making plans. Breaking that habit and not thinking any further than the next hour, or meal time, is a challenge but it can often be the only way to survive grief in the first few months.

Yet amongst all these feelings of fear and confusion, you are expected to sit down and make serious decisions about financial matters, fill in forms correctly, wait in telephone holding queues with call centres for hours on end and then not break down in tears or lose your rag with someone who says they absolutely have to talk to your dead partner – or worse that he needs to write to them in person.

I cried on the phone to my bank, with a financial advisor, when phoning the RAC. With every phone call you make it is as if you are erasing more of the person you love, taking their name off documents, rubbing out their identity bit by bit. It's a gruelling experience to have to go through.

Three years after Nick died I was still getting two sets of bills in his name – I just never got round to changing them and it was comforting to see post with his name come through the door. It reminded me that he had been here, helped me sort things out, took charge of some of the household responsibilities and that we had been a team. I didn't want to erase him completely.

Only now do I feel that I have reached the end of the to do list he left on his desk when he died.

Can you, as a friend or relative, actually make any of this easier? Even without knowing intimate details of your friend's financial situation there are still many things you can help take care of.

Here are some suggestions:

- Register the death for your friend, and when you do, get at least 10 copies of the death certificate to send to all the people who will request one.

- Offer to deal with some of the letter writing. You can write to all the utilities, phone companies etc giving details of the death, enclosing a death certificate and asking for a change of name. All your friend will have to do is sign the letters.

- Write to the pension funds her partner was a member of enclosing a death certificate to put the pension claim in motion.

- Find out which benefits your friend is entitled to and help fill in the forms. You can order a bereavement benefits claim pack, Form BB1, from your nearest JobCentre Plus or social security office. See www.direct.gov.uk for more information.

- Accompany your friend when they have to go to the Job Centre, social security office, bank etc. Moral support can be very encouraging when dealing with officials and you may be thinking more clearly and better able to answer questions or retain information.

- Help your friend write a list of everything that needs to be dealt with and sort items into 'urgent' and 'later'.

- Write to the local council – your friend will now be eligible for a 25% reduction in council tax payments if he/she is now the sole adult living in the house.

- Inform the car insurance company – if the surviving spouse is insured under their partner's name they may not be legally insured to drive.

- Ask your friend to put aside mail that arrives for their partner so you can see what still needs to be dealt with. Often subscriptions and memberships for clubs, magazines etc will turn up weeks or months later – things you didn't know about or have completely forgotten. There may be Direct Debits that haven't been stopped and are costing money.

- Driving licences should be sent back to the DVLA in Swansea and Blue Badges (disabled driver/passenger permits) to the local authority.

- Some Blue Badge owners are exempt from paying car tax. If the badge is returned, the car will need to be retaxed and a new disc displayed in the windscreen.

- Passports should be sent back to the UK Passport Agency.

- Order books and girocheques should be sent back to the relevant social security office. Keep a record of book numbers before sending anything back.

- Season tickets should be returned – refunds may be due. Sports club memberships need to be cancelled.

- NHS equipment such as walking aids, wheelchairs and artificial limbs should be returned.

- If you have any specialist knowledge, don't be afraid to offer to share it with a bereaved friend. If you are a solicitor you may be able to help with the legalities of closing down a business or winding up an estate. You may be able to help resolve problems with children, children-in-law or an ex-partner or spouse. If no Will was left by the deceased then your friend will need help to try and unravel the knots and sort out what to do with the estate. Don't be shy about offering your help, though they may feel such issues are private and want to deal with them alone. Make clear that you are willing to answer any questions without going into the specifics of their own particular circumstances.

- If you are an expert in accounts or tax, your knowledge might come in handy when dealing with financial affairs. If the deceased was self-employed it can be tricky to tie up all the loose ends and you may be able to help by thinking clearly and knowing all the different areas that need to be looked at.

- If you are less emotionally involved it can be easier to deal with the intricacies, frustrations and delays that come with the bureaucracy surrounding death. You will have more distance and clarity than someone who is newly bereaved and may spot problems or solutions more easily than them. But be aware that dealing with some of the bureaucracy can be hard for best friends and close family too, so before you step in and offer to take over an important task make sure you are up to doing it.

The insanity of bureaucracy

"I had a four month old baby and a two year old and my world had just fallen apart. I still feel angry that the system was so inflexible and that I was treated so insensitively. Sometimes it took an almost superhuman effort to sit at my desk and plough through the interminable tasks. Looking back three years on, I really don't know how I did it, and much of it I can't remember – it was just an awful dark place I never want to revisit and wouldn't wish on my worst enemy."

"The admin I had to deal with after Jonathan's death was just horrendous. I could have predicted the other things that were thrown at me: the grief, shock, etc. But I would have had no idea that I would be stuck in paperwork hell for a good six months to a year after his death. I remember a particularly depressing visit to Hoxton social security office, in order to get widow's benefit, where I had to wait with everyone else there claiming benefits and then explain to a deaf and insensitive official exactly what had happened through a sheet of bullet proof glass. I felt extremely lonely."

"I went to see my local MP about the way the DSS treated me. I was sat in the main waiting area with drug addicts and alcoholics whilst two people that were in for defrauding were taken into a nice secluded office. I had to sit in public while everyone around heard me crying and trying to explain everything to the bereavement officer."

"I was totally lost with all the paperwork and also the red tape involved when you are at your most vulnerable. And why has everything got to be done so quickly? But then the response is so slow?"

"As an accountant the financial side/paperwork was not a problem, although I found the benefit forms unbelievably complicated and their helplines less than helpful. Some of the insurance companies were also less than helpful, and their staff not overly sensitive. One of them did ask to speak to my wife even though they knew I was processing a life insurance claim!"

"I did have horrible conversations with some life assurance companies. One young man just cut me off when I told him that my husband was no longer here. When I called back his colleague took the call but she already knew the story. I was very hurt and angry."

"If someone could have come in and seen to everything all in one go it would have been wonderful. I think I would have gladly paid for it

all! But as soon as you thought you'd completed one form there would be something else returned as incomplete or more information required. I was quite overwhelmed."

"Unfortunately a family member offered to do the inheritance tax forms for me, perhaps not realising what a complicated and emotionally difficult task that can be for someone close to the one who has died, and a year on, things hadn't progressed. It was like a huge cloud hanging over us and in the end I had to step in and pass it on to a solicitor. "

"We were in the process of remortgaging, so our home was in fact unsecured and my earnings didn't cover the repayments on paper, so I thought we might lose the house. It took hundreds of calls to sort out – all clouded by anger: why hadn't the lawyers sorted it out properly when they were supposed to, the week before he died? Why hadn't we ticked the box for life insurance? I now know that that anger is all to do with grief, and is a sort of floating rage - but there are many, many outlets for it in admin hell."

"There was a mountain of admin to do with the mortgage, his social security – so that I could get widow's benefit or whatever it's called… It was particularly difficult because this is the one point in your life when you are least able to deal with insensitive phone operators, mindless bureaucrats and endless depressing hours banging your head against a brick wall trying to sort things out. I found myself having to explain over and over again what had happened, and having conversations that made me feel like I was going mad."

"Some things remain unsorted – the post still in his name, and Sky TV cables still hang out of the wall – but everything important got done. About a year ago, I reviewed the rolling to do list that had *plagued me since his death, and just struck off a lot of things that were still outstanding – I'll never claim back the insurance he had paid twice, and I've given up trying to find out if I'm getting as much social security benefit on his pension payments as I should. A few things I wish I had done – I let his email account expire without printing out or looking through all his messages, some of which I had wanted to save for the children because his personality shone through in them. I wish I had done that – I hadn't realised they would one day just expire into the ether just like he had, if I didn't keep the account active. But I know why I didn't – it was just too painful and I had too much on my plate trying to earn money and cope, so I have learned to be very forgiving of myself."*

"My husband spent days trying to sort out insurance for the last holiday we went on. He had terminal cancer so the usual companies wouldn't touch him. With the help of Macmillan he eventually found a policy, which was incredibly expensive, but we were convinced we had to have it. We went to France and three days into our luxury holiday – no expense spared as we knew it would be our last – he told me we had to leave that day, otherwise he'd never make it home. The company were fantastic and flew us back immediately without question. Nick died 36 hours after reaching Gatwick. I never claimed on the insurance policy that he had spent so long trying to sort out – somehow it got lost in the midst of dealing with his death and arranging a funeral and it really didn't seem important at the time. But I realised later that the girls and I might have had a good holiday out of what could have been paid out for that trip. If someone had dealt with that for me it could have come in really handy, but we just didn't think of doing it."

"It took two years to resolve Ian's estate, wind up his company and sort probate. I fortunately had a good accountant friend and a superb

solicitor, free of charge. It was frightening to consider all the paper-work, it seemed endless. I had no idea what to do."

"There was a never ending barrage of letters from the Inland Revenue – you'll get this benefit, then a letter saying how much they'll tax you on it; then because of the benefit your tax code is going to change; then his tax return; then your tax return; then another benefit; then a pension payment; then another change of tax code. It was a never ending spiral. I had no idea of what I was actually getting and how long for. It felt like whatever I was being given was being taken away again. Why couldn't they deal with it all and then send you a summary of your entitlements?"

"The government could make some of this so much easier. They should make sure that when you register a death you receive a pack with all the information you need. You might not be entitled to all the benefits but it could at the very least act as a checklist."

"As I have always done the family finances I simply carried on, but it was tremendously draining emotionally, not least because most of these institutions haven't the slightest idea how to respond to someone saying 'I'm phoning because my husband has died'. Responses ranged from 'Oh' to 'Well, what do you want me to do?' Rarely was there a spark of humanity at the other end of the line."

"After Penny died the battery in her mobile was flat and I couldn't turn it back on without a password – I wanted to get access to the photos and text messages on it as well as contact numbers for notify-ing people. I took it to Carphone Warehouse who said they could not do anything about it unless I reregistered the phone in my name. I said, OK fine, thinking I could pay for a month and then cancel the contract. Of course three months later, when I finally get round to

doing that, it transpires I have signed up for a year without realising it. I wrote to the company explaining what had happened and saying a) I thought I had been mis-sold the contract and b) they should have some arrangement for situations like that. They basically responded – tough, you signed, you have to pay and started threatening legal action. It took me about six months to sort it out and I'm sure it only finally got resolved when I alerted the press office that I had written to the chairman Charles Dunstone."

"Immediately before Iestyn died I tidied up the main utilities bills by transferring them to my account from his. Simple I thought. I had just told British Gas that he was now in a coma and days, maybe hours, away from death – and their response was that he had to telephone them to deal with this as I couldn't. I said no, you don't understand, he's unconscious he can't phone you himself and the woman replied 'well he'll have to write in then!'"

"I became obsessed about dealing with my own financial affairs in case I died as well – I sorted out bills, accounts, savings, my own Will, it became a frantic obsession about a month after Ian's death, so nobody would have to go through the financial nightmare I had had to."

Money
(What people never talk about until you are widowed)

It's a certainty that your friend's financial situation will change following the death of the person they lived with – for better or worse. Some widowed people find themselves set up for life with no need to worry about money again – but this is rare. In the research for this book I've only come across one or two people who fall into that category. For the rest, the future is a much more uncertain creature than it once was.

In 2003, nearly 8,000 women and 3,500 men in their thirties and forties were widowed. That's a lot of people dealing with a sea change in their financial circumstances at what is traditionally the highest earning period in a working life.

Insurance payouts or not, the bereaved partner either has to survive on what they've inherited, or somehow compensate for the lost earnings of a partner. Pensions don't pay out a great deal if you've only contributed to them for 10 or 15 years.

For a woman widowed at 60, she knows she may well live for another 20 years and may never have dealt with finances before. It can be a frightening prospect and many older women are scared they will not have enough money to last. In 2003, 30,000 women were widowed in their sixties compared to 12,000 men, so it is a situation women face far more often (statistics only record numbers for married couples).

Widowed parents may not be able to work full time because of the logistics or cost of childcare and the future can look quite intimidating. Further education costs money and older children often need a helping hand to get set up on leaving home.

Bereaved fathers can feel strong pressure to keep working full time and may be scared about losing the identity that comes with a job, particularly after losing a wife. However if she did the lion's share of childcare, then holding down a full time job could suddenly involve paying serious money for childcare after school and in holidays if there is not extended family around who can help.

Bereaved people also often end up having to pay for help with jobs around the home that their partner would have taken care of, for example gardening, DIY, car maintenance, washing windows, etc.

It's important to try and be tactful when it comes to financial affairs. Here are some pointers:

- Don't assume a widow(er) is automatically rich. Even if there was a life insurance payout there are still ongoing expenses to cover and they may have lost the main breadwinner in the family or the only income.

- A lump sum payment has to be enormous to set someone up for life and it's extremely unlikely your friend will have received anything like enough never to have to worry about money again.

- There are likely to be more expenses in running the household from now on.

- Don't ask someone who has been widowed about their financial situation unless it's something you would have talked about before. Several people I barely knew asked me whether my mortgage had been paid off – not one of them would have asked me something like that before Nick died and I was staggered people could be so insensitive.

- Try not to pass comment on how your widowed friend spends their money – there may be more to it than meets the eye.

"A colleague at work once said to me 'Well at least your mortgage has been paid off'! Yes, it's one less thing to worry about. But no, I wouldn't rather have my house than my husband."

"The most annoying comment I have received is in relation to the mortgage – a number of people have said how good it must feel to have no mortgage, and my response has sometimes been that I would gladly double the mortgage if it meant Jo was still alive."

"I'm amazed at how many people believe that if you have no mortgage you never have to worry about money again. But if you've lost two-thirds of your household income how are you supposed to pay all the other bills? The university costs, insurance premiums, utilities, car expenses? Unlike many of our friends we'd never taken out a crazy mortgage so that payment was only ever a small part of our outgoings. Everything else still has to be paid for and I do find it hard. But because I don't have that one payment to make everyone seems to think I don't have a care in the world – if only that were so."

"Everyone assumes that I am left comfortably off. If I had not been, I think it might have been quite difficult because I go out for lots of meals and drive the car to many places. This is all lovely but it costs a lot of money and I am lucky to be able to agree to everything that is suggested. I don't think that any friends question that I cannot manage."

"I long to give up work and be with our son… No chance of that now, I am the only breadwinner. Yes, I could give up work and claim benefits but my pride won't let me. I have to prove to myself that I can do it and make my husband proud of me."

"I bought myself a rather fast little sports car after David died and some people made nasty comments about how I was wasting my money and how I was being disrespectful. What they didn't realise was that David and I had always dreamed of having this car and he wanted me to have it. I know he would have been really pleased to see me driving it and enjoying myself after what we'd been through."

"My family thinks I am financially fortunate and should be grateful. They don't seem to understand that any life insurance is a poor second to continuing income. And I am sure it costs the same to run a house with one adult as two, if not more when I have to pay for babysitting and help with the gardening."

"I might have a lump sum sitting in the bank at the moment, but my mortgage hasn't been paid off, I have a monthly nursery bill, I still need to work full time to make ends meet. What happens if I'm off long term sick? How am I going to put my son through university? What about all those unexpected bills and repairs? How long will that money last and what is it really worth in today's terms?"

"Never assume that a widow is wealthy… not everyone has insurance and I was deeply upset by comments to the effect of 'Oh you'll be alright now the mortgage can be paid off' and 'Lucky you' when I got my widow's allowance cheque for £2,000. Lucky me? Oh yes, I've just lost the man I loved more than anything else in the world, but I've got £2,000 to pay for his funeral. That's alright then."

GOLDEN RULES:

- Ask if you can write some letters to deal with name changes, pensions etc.

- Offer help if you are professionally qualified eg solicitor, tax advisor.

- Accompany your friend to social security offices, banks etc.

- Help your friend write a checklist of everything that needs to be done.

- Remember that the bureaucracy lasts for months after a death, not a few days.

- Don't assume your friend has come into serious money.

CHAPTER FIVE

Getting away from it all

I used to love holidays. I have a reputation of always having dreadful weather wherever I go, but despite that travelling was something I really enjoyed whether it was camping, lazing around on beaches or enjoying a nice hotel.

But then Nick got sick. Two weeks before our longed for two week summer holiday in Greece with friends he went into hospital and despite our hopes that he'd be out in a couple of days and right as rain to go away, it didn't happen.

During his illness we tried several times to have a break and he was either too ill to go or, as happened once, we went and he ended up in a cancer ward in hospital somewhere far from home where I knew no one. It didn't seem worth it in the end. Our last trip away together was reduced to one night after another emergency hospital visit and I remember sitting in the restaurant of a lovely hotel in Dorset while Nick tried to convince me he was enjoying his dinner when he could barely eat. We discussed his funeral – there was little else on our minds.

Nick was determined to make it back to France, which he loved, before he died. On June 18th 2003 we headed to Bordeaux with the children. He had been extremely tired in the run up to the trip, a sign we'd been told that would mean his liver was failing. But he rested a lot the previous week and was determined to go. We arrived in our luxury chalet on Wednesday evening and the girls were delighted with the swimming pool. Nick's nerves were shattered as he sat watching Laura, 17 months, running at full tilt out of the house, across the patio and straight into the pool – with me following closely behind. He couldn't move quickly enough to catch her and was terrified at what might happen. We quickly shut the patio doors.

We had a happy couple of days – Nick slept a lot and ate little but the girls played around him and he watched them spend happy hours in the pool and cycling around with me – or rather riding a trailer like queens while I pedalled furiously in front.

On Saturday lunchtime they were having lunch in a children's club and I came back for a much needed rest. He told me we had to go home that day otherwise he wouldn't make it back from France. I didn't believe him – or rather couldn't accept what I was hearing – but he insisted he knew what was happening. After some very difficult phone calls and rushed packing, we left for the airport and made it back to Gatwick late that evening, the girls a little bemused at why they'd been whisked out of the kids' club and straight to the airport by the holiday nanny…

Nick died 36 hours after our plane landed.

Family holidays have never been the same since. They used to be a time when we went away together, spent precious time playing and relaxing, enjoying each other's company and discovering new things about one other. We'd only had a couple of trips as a foursome but we'd had wonderful holidays as a couple and then with Ellie before Laura came along.

Years later, holidays are still a reminder of what's missing and I face them with dread. Planning them alone isn't nearly as much fun – gone is the enjoyable anticipation of a shared trip. And when the time comes I have to sort out the house and cat, pack for us all, remember everything, lock up, face a long drive or manage two kids and luggage at airports or train stations. After a long journey I then have to cope with two excited children who want to run straight into the garden/sea/swimming pool while at the same time unpacking the car and doing all the usual sorting out you do on arrival…

We're beginning to learn what works for us as a family, as other widows and widowers do too, but it takes time to get used to this new reality. The holiday industry is so heavily biased towards couples and nuclear families that there's really nothing quite like it to emphasise your loss.

It's a cruel twist that one of the things that used to bring you joy, help you unwind and enable you to leave some of your worries behind now seems to do just the opposite – it reinforces your new found situation and can make you feel even more lonely than you do when you're able to subsume yourself in your daily routine at home.

Holidays can be even harder later in life – when you are just beginning to make the most of having more free time and holidaying together without children. The travelling companion, along with a lifetime's holiday plans, is now gone, and travelling alone can be a very unappealing prospect.

So how can you make this precious and difficult time of year better for someone who has lost the one person they want to share their holidays with?

- Offer to go away with your widowed parent for a few days, just the two of you, without the grandchildren. It gives your parent a good opportunity to talk, to share memories of a loved partner/parent and they will appreciate the opportunity to spend time with you.

- Encourage an older widowed friend or relative to take a trip with another widowed or single friend – it could well be easier for them than going away alone or with a couple.

- For younger widowed parents, going away with friends can be the best option – it's a way of sharing the workload and enjoying some adult company. Be aware that it could feel awkward for your bereaved friend if you used to go away together before and be ready to step in and help with childcare, particularly when your friend is unpacking, pitching a tent, cooking a meal or similar.

- Invite your friend for short visits – weekend trips or overnight stays. It's good to have something to look forward to and having more shorter trips away rather than one long holiday can be a good way to relieve loneliness.

- Short breaks are easier for everyone to cope with, especially if your friend is feeling particularly vulnerable, low or emotional.

- Be prepared to see more of a widowed parent than you did before, particularly at holiday times of year.

- Invite your friend to join you for part of your summer holiday. That way you still have time with your own family but your friend will feel loved and wanted. When you've lost your partner you can feel like a huge burden on everyone else and you are aware that people may find your company quite exhausting. Knowing that people still want to be your friend and spend time with you is very valuable, but bereaved people are aware that your holiday is important to you too and they won't want to intrude.

- Try to arrange something new or interesting to do with a bereaved friend. While lying around sleeping may be what they need to do to restore lost energy, it can be very hard to relax and do nothing when you're worried, stressed or depressed. Exercise, sightseeing or travelling will all help focus their mind on something else and be a good way to escape for a while. I had a wonderful week in Morocco with two very close friends two years after Nick died. It was the perfect holiday – not too expensive, lovely weather, a short flight and plenty to see and do. Riding a donkey in the mountains and haggling in the souks was such fun it really took my mind of what had happened for a while.

- Offer to look after children so your friend can have a break. Many parents won't want to leave their children straight away but after a few months it is important for them to find more time for themselves and they may be more willing then to leave the children with a trusted friend or relative.

- Offer to take children on day trips during school holidays. That way they don't have to leave their parents overnight but it will give the parent a much needed break.

- Ring up on the spur of the moment if you've decided to go somewhere and could invite your friend along. Newly bereaved people can often only manage to think one or two days ahead and may not have made plans for weekends or bank holidays. If they're busy then ask again on another occasion. Remember that even a year or two on from their bereavement, holidays will still be tricky and they'll appreciate being invited to spend time with you.

- Be careful about how you talk about your own holidays – your friend may not be that interested in how fantastic your latest trip is going to be, or how difficult it is to agree with your partner on where to go. Those conversations only serve to remind them what they've lost and it could be a couple of years before they're able to discuss things like this with you without feeling sad, angry or resentful.

How it feels

"Any regular, normal holiday is utter torture."

"For five years since my wife became ill I haven't looked forward to a holiday, and haven't even wanted to plan one. I get angry in spring when my friends start planning their annual trips and talking about them."

"We had our retirement trips all planned… we were going to explore Italy together and we had both dreamed of going on a safari one day too. I know I'll never do those things now – even though I could go it just wouldn't be the same, and sharing it was the whole point. The dreams died the day I lost Mary."

"I was sitting on the beach one day this summer when I saw a man, around my age, walking up the beach with his two daughters. One, who must have been about four, walked beside him carefully holding two ice creams. He carried the other, younger child in his arm, gleefully holding her own ice cream. It could have been Robert. My heart broke all over again."

"What I really hate is when friends tell me enthusiastically about the holidays they are going on, then ask what I'm doing as if I'm going to be just as enthusiastic about mine. How can I possibly be? Don't they realise I will never go on holiday again with the only person I want to?"

"With holidays I've been lucky. A friend, also in her sixties, was going though a divorce at the same time as my bereavement and we holidayed together."

"My children are grown-up now and live in the south and when I go to them it is like a holiday because I am so spoiled and they organise all sorts of outings and treats."

"I feel that future holidays will need to be with a singles organisation. I do not think I could cope with any one friend for a long period of time and that in many ways I would be better with strangers and a bit of adventure – we will see."

"We'd booked a family holiday, the three of us and my parents, six months before it happened. The holiday was two weeks after Stewart died. My Mum took control of everything – first she cancelled it, then she thought it would be a good idea and cancelled the cancellation. We had to take my husband's car, it was the only one big enough for us all to fit in, so I ended up driving everywhere. Seeing the car was a constant reminder to both me and my two year old… I felt trapped and so alone. Being with them, as a couple, made me miss my husband even more and they seemed oblivious to this."

"Holidays are something that are needed but are to be dreaded too, as they encapsulate all your best memories, and now, guess what, you're on your own. No one to share with, no one to get the suitcases off the conveyor belt, no one to share the bottle of wine with, hold hands with, rub sun cream on your back, I could go on…"

"Everyone else is in wonderful little happy families, like salt in the wounds, sussing you out and wondering how your husband could have run off with another woman and left you on your own with a baby."

"I was very lucky in the first year to be able to go away with two other girlfriends… it was a good way to face the dragons of a first time abroad without your other half. It was brave of my friends, as holidays are precious and for them a newly bereaved widow isn't exactly a bundle of laughs, and I am very grateful to them for that."

"I hate the thought of taking holidays. For the past two summers, the first without my husband, I have taken odd days off work and gone to stay with old friends dotted around the country and they have been very successful; kids and all getting on. But the thought of going just the four of us terrifies me."

"I have thought of asking friends to come with us but I don't want to be a pity case and I fear they'll come without really wanting to. If I had what I thought to be a genuine invitation to go with another family I enjoyed the company of, I would jump at it."

"My worst holiday was in Croyde Bay, on my own, with the children. I will never do that again."

"We've been invited to join friends on holidays – part success, part failure. It was a success when we went with a family and each day we decided what we were going to do together. It was a failure when we were told what the family were doing and we could take it or leave it – I felt bored and lonely! Bank holidays are long and lonely."

"Our best trips by far have been with a family we know really well. We've been to beaches in Devon and Wales and gone skiing together too. The children adore each other and I get on really well with both husband and wife and somehow they never make me feel like a spare part. I wish we could share all our holidays but obviously they want to go away without us sometimes too!"

"In Greece I realised I needed to rethink the holiday situation, because the evening time in the bar was as lonely as hell."

"I have one friend who keeps complaining about how hard it is to find a holiday that suits her and her husband. One of them wants fully inclusive, the other wants to explore local restaurants… it's so hard to find the perfect destination. I can't tell her how much it hurts me to listen, I'd much rather she moaned about it to someone else. If only she could just think about how lucky she is to have a husband to plan a trip with – and go away with. I wouldn't care where I ate dinner if I could eat it with my husband."

GOLDEN RULES:

- Try and invite your friend to join you on a holiday or short trip.

- Involve other people so it's not just you in a couple and your widowed friend.

- Don't expect your friend to enjoy holidays in the same way, but know that they will appreciate the change, a rest and your company.

- Go away with a widowed parent for a few days, without the grandchildren if possible. It's a chance for them to talk and share memories.

- Take one or more of your friend's children away for a few days so they can have some fun and your friend can rest.

- Be sensitive about how you talk about your own trips and holidays.

CHAPTER SIX

The never ending to do list

The 'little things' in life can often be overwhelming for someone who is newly bereaved. Being faced with a job that was something your partner always took care of, or a task that can only be done by two people, is a constant reminder of the person you have lost. It can also be the straw that breaks the camel's back when you're trying really hard to hold it all together and keep going.

There are many bits and pieces of life that can be a bit too much for a bereaved person to cope with including DIY, gardening, car maintenance, shopping, driving and various other chores.

When someone loses a partner they may have lost the person who did the gardening, or cooked the meals. They may be faced with tasks they have no experience of or are bewildered by. For older people particularly it can be daunting to have to think of taking on these jobs, especially at a time when they are feeling vulnerable and exhausted.

Paying for odd-job men to come in and do little tasks is impractical and expensive – many workmen won't consider doing odd jobs and many widows and widowers simply couldn't afford it anyway. Bereaved women may be especially nervous of asking strangers into the house to fix things.

So here are some ideas for things that friends and neighbours can do to make life a little easier. Some are obvious, some are things you wouldn't think would become a problem. But bereavement is exhausting – just getting through the day can be enough of a challenge for weeks, if not months. The practical jobs involved in keeping a house running can, quite simply, be too much to cope with.

Those who have children also find themselves in a situation where it is impossible to get anything practical done – weekends are spent single handedly going to the park, swimming, driving to football practice or supervising homework. Where once one parent would do that while the other cut the grass or put up a shelf, now you have to deal with the kids alone all day and then try and get the jobs done once they're in bed, you're shattered and you still haven't done the washing, opened the post or answered your phone messages.

I have never been afraid of DIY and though I'm no expert, have reasonably successfully sanded floors, fixed a broken washing machine and built a hundred bits of Ikea furniture. I have my own toolbox and frankly Nick didn't even know what was in it. So this has never been a case of 'I don't have a man around the house to fix things any more', but rather a case of having been so exhausted that a broken shower or unexpected car problem has often felt like it could finally push me over the edge.

What can you do?

Sit down with your friend and write a list of all the things that need doing, from mowing the lawn to fixing the puncture in a bicycle tyre. Stick the list on their fridge, or somewhere obvious where all visitors to the house will see it.

Next time someone says 'Is there anything I can do?' all they need to do is point to the list and say 'Yes, actually, loads of things. Pick something off that list – anything you fancy.'

Why does this work?

- English people get embarrassed. They hate asking anyone to do anything.

- This way the bereaved person doesn't have to ask her visitor outright to do something for her.

- She doesn't run the risk of asking someone to do something they can't, or would really hate to do.

- Her visitors can pick something they are happy to do and have the know-how to manage, and they can then get on with the job they've chosen.

Everybody's happy – no one's embarrassed.

In the absence of such a list existing on your friend's fridge door, here are some suggestions:

Gardening

- Draw up a rota amongst neighbours for mowing the lawn – once a week in summer, less often in winter. Each of you will only have to do it a few times a year but it will remove a huge headache from a tired, bereaved neighbour. Make sure the lawnmower is in good, working condition. If it isn't, repair it or arrange to have it repaired – don't just tell your neighbour it's broken and leave them to get it fixed.

- Cut your neighbour's hedge once a year or offer to do some pruning.

- Plant some bulbs in the winter so they have something pretty to look at in spring – and it could be a nice surprise for them, if they don't want to specify what you put in.

- Offer to fix a broken fence or squeaking gate – these are little jobs that may only take you a few hours, but every time a friend sees the results they will feel people are taking care of them and will appreciate your help enormously.

- If the gardener of the house has died, and you are good at gardening, offer to show your friend how to do some basic jobs so they will feel empowered and a little more able to cope with something their partner always took care of.

- If your friend always worked in the garden with his wife, then suggest you work on it together. It will be nice for him to have some company and satisfying to get a job done while having a chat at the same time.

DIY

- If you're good at DIY visit your friend and ask what needs doing. Tell them when you have free time and say you'd be happy to spend a day or two doing odd jobs. Offer again in six months' time when other things will need doing.

- If you're visiting and see light bulbs that aren't working or taps that are dripping, offer to fix them there and then. Taking control and getting on with a job can be very effective – it means the bereaved person doesn't have to ask you again if you forget to come back and they will know that you care enough to want to help. But do ask before getting out your spanners.

- Check doors and windows have adequate locks – newly bereaved people who are suddenly living on their own, possibly for the first time in decades, can feel extremely vulnerable.

- Help turn a double mattress over.

- Put things up in the loft or get things down.

- Hang pictures or mirrors – impossible to do on your own especially if they're big.

- Check and change batteries in smoke alarms regularly.

Cars and bikes

- If you're good with cars make this 'your' job. Offer to check oil, water, tyres etc or fill up the car with antifreeze when it gets cold.

- If you know your friend is about to go on a long car journey, offer to check the car over first.

- Remind your friend about servicing the car or offer to take it to the garage. Remembering to deal with such things can be very low down the to do list for a bereaved person – having someone to lift this burden can be extremely helpful.

- Offer to check children's bikes and fix punctures etc.

- Bereaved people have to do the driving. The deal over who can have a drink and who drives home is no longer an option.

So offer to drive – pick your friend up and drop them home after a social gathering – they'll be relieved to be able to have a drink and it will help them to relax. Socialising can be extremely hard for newly bereaved people and often a drink will help them enjoy themselves. Remember that if you drive a bereaved person to a party or social occasion they may hate it and want to come home after half an hour – tell them you'll be happy to do this and then be prepared to do it with a smile. (You could always go back later.)

- If your friend's partner died in a traffic accident be extra aware that they may need some help with driving for quite a while afterwards – offer them lifts if you go the same way, and offer to drive any children around too.

Computers

- If you know about computers offer to help keep an eye on things like antivirus software and backing up precious files.

- The computer can be a lifeline for people suddenly living on their own – if grown-up children are far away, for example, the computer can serve as a great way to stay in touch with children and grandchildren. If it crashes, or gets a virus, not only does it suddenly mean the bereaved person is out of touch with others, but it can mean the loss of valuable letters, photos and other memories.

- Use your skills to show your friend how to do basic tasks on the computer if they haven't used one before. It is empowering to learn new skills and shows them they can achieve things on their own.

- If the person who died worked on a home computer, and you are confident enough to do this safely, offer to back up their work and store it properly so nothing will be lost if the computer crashes. Make more than one copy so your friend can be confident nothing will be lost.

- Ask your friend whether they'd like you to copy or print out their partner's emails – once an email account expires these will be lost forever.

- If you're not confident enough to do any of this reliably, organise for a professional who you know and trust to come in and do it for your friend.

- Help connect printers, digital camera software, home networks etc and spend the time explaining how they work. Not only will it save your friend serious money in getting professionals in, but will give them more confidence in knowing how to use their own equipment.

Miscellaneous

- If your friend is struggling to keep on top of things help do some general household chores. Don't just pop in, drink tea and leave. Offer to sort some washing while you chat, help put clean clothes away or do some ironing. Pick things up, stack or empty the dishwasher, get rid of the junk mail. Make it clear you're not passing comment on the state of the house, but just want to lend a hand.

- Offer to look after a pet when your friend goes away.

- Offer to take your friend to an airport or train station, or to collect them after a trip.

- If you live next door, pop out when your friend returns from a trip and help with the luggage, deal with tired children or make a cup of tea. Returning alone from a trip or holiday to an empty house can be quite traumatic after bereavement and having someone there for half an hour to chat to makes a huge difference.

- If you are staying with a bereaved friend, make sure your visit doesn't create more work. Help cook the meals or do the shopping and change your bed linen when you leave so the room is ready for someone else.

- As new school terms approach you could offer to buy extra school uniforms if you're getting them for your own children, or take children shopping for shoes. Offer to sew in name tapes, write names in uniform or do mending.

How to offer

It's tricky to strike the balance between being helpful and interfering in a way that makes a friend feel they have no control of their life. But a good rule of thumb is that if you notice something needs fixing or looks like it might break or is dangerous, your friend has probably noticed it too.

Say you've seen something that needs fixing and offer to do it. 'Those bulbs have gone - would you like me to come round tomorrow and replace them?' All that requires is a relieved 'Yes, please' and the job's done. No toes are trodden on, no one is insulted. And what's more, your friend won't feel they're imposing on your time and goodwill because you offered in the first place.

How people feel

"Let me know if there's anything I can do' is not the helpful offer it seems. We hear it a lot. If you really want to help, start asking 'is there anything that needs doing?', and really work at getting the answers. The bereaved person probably has lots of small things that need doing, but feels unable or unwilling to ask... Also, they may feel totally unable to focus on what jobs need doing, so it's a great help to have someone make a cup of tea and sit down with pen and paper to work out what needs doing when."

"My overall experience has been that the most helpful people are those who get on and do something, rather than just offer vaguely, although maybe this is partly because I'm so bad at asking for help."

"One of the most helpful short term things someone did was a friend who organised (and paid for) a builder to come and fix my gutter which was falling down. A friend of Mike's also offered to ring round to cancel his work commitments."

"I needed some electric work done and I went to Care and Repair which is a charitable organisation that has volunteers to do tasks for older people. I didn't want that sort of help, but I wanted to go to electricians that could be trusted. They were happy to give me two names."

"One friend helped me to assign tasks for other friends. It would have been impossible to do by myself and rather lonely. This was much more enjoyable. We simply went through all the kinds of things I needed doing, drew up a list of all the friends who would be willing to be asked to help for things, and worked out who could do what."

"The everyday routines – you cut the lawn, he strimmed it; you loaded the dishwasher, he unloaded it; you got the kids dressed, he did the packed lunches; he dropped them off at nursery, you picked them up. How do you cope with it all on your own? You get in help (friends, family, employ somebody), but then you resent the help because they don't do it like you do it; you feel like you are a failure by not being able to do it all yourself."

"Buying a new car on my own was a nightmare. You feel you are at the mercy of these men who are rubbing their hands in glee seeing a lone woman walking into the showroom. I am always very aware that I never get the same service or attitude as a woman in any area dominated by males, car showrooms and building supply merchants to name just a couple."

"A friend has tried to persuade me to employ a group of male Polish workers to do some gardening work. I will not, but people don't understand that I cannot behave in the same way as they do. I must sound paranoid, but I'm not."

"When I said no thanks to help with practical tasks, it was because I felt a failure at not coping, not that I didn't want the help!"

"Initially people could not help me enough, but now I would have to ask and some women are not happy about their men helping me. I did not believe this would happen but it has."

"A light bulb at the top of the stairs went unchanged for around a year until I propped a ladder up there and could barely reach even on tiptoes at full stretch. It was highly dangerous, but whenever I said this to my taller friends, the response was always the same: 'Yes, it is a long way up, isn't it?'"

"Several people offered to fix my lawn mower and would ask from time to time, 'Lawn mower fixed yet?' 'No.' 'I'll be round to fix it next week.' I don't know why I didn't fix it sooner, but I felt a great sense of pride when I finally achieved it myself."

"*The week Michael died my bath tap started dripping and now over two years later it's still the same. I asked several friends for help and it was always 'I'll come and look next week', but here I am still waiting. It got to the point where I stopped asking people for help as they never did it anyway and it's not that I wanted it doing for nothing, I always offered to pay them for it. They really should not offer to help just because they feel obliged to, because when it comes down to it they never carry it out anyway.*"

"I have learned to ask. People are generally very happy to be asked."

"*Ron did all the cutting of the grass and hedges in the garden and I did the weeding. I now do it all. I had a man who is the gardener for my neighbours to do the hedges and other heavy things but he was coming in without telling me and then sending quite a large bill. I felt I had to put a stop to that… I have found it better to persevere myself as I can actually manage quite a lot… I am amazed at what I can manage.*"

"I hated the phrase 'remember we are here for you – whenever you need help'. I just wished friends would phone rather than me having to phone them for help. It was just so hard asking for help."

"*It's hard to accept 'favours' such as lifts to and from school, or after school care, without feeling one should be reciprocating – which is how it usually works amongst parents. But I know that I'm doing all I can at present just surviving, and in the future I hope I'll have a chance to help someone out in these invaluable small ways.*"

"The most unhelpful are people who offer help and don't come through with it, like the friend's husband who said if there was anything he could do around the house, to let him know. Then when I asked if he could put a curtain rail up for me, he said 'I'll tell you how to do it, but I haven't got time.'"

"When I was having some work done on my central heating system a friend offered to, and then wrote out, a list of everything I should check before accepting the estimate. He also came round half way through the job and talked to the man to make sure he was doing the right thing – that made me feel much more confident."

"It's a pain to have to rely on someone else to do the smallest of things, especially on moving into a house. Things like changing light fittings, assembling beds; heavy things that you have to rely on others' strength for, is very frustrating."

"For months I would go downstairs at night and not be able to see anything because so many of the lightbulbs had gone – it was really quite dangerous."

"The computer was one of my phobias – I'm happy in my own world but once something goes wrong, eg the printer stops working, a virus appears or any of the jargon that goes along with IT makes me a quivering wreck… Setting up an Internet account is a nightmare to the novice… I had friends I could call on but after a while I would get conscious that they might get fed up too."

"I have adjusted my expectations so for example, the car very rarely gets washed, whereas I would do this quite frequently before. The grass is longer than it would be and the garden has gone to pot. Fewer things are ironed than used to be."

GOLDEN RULES:

- Offer to do jobs around the house and garden that you can manage and that need doing – don't wait for your friend to ask.

- Offer to find other people to do jobs you can't – someone will be good at computers, someone else at gardening, cars, DIY or cooking.

- If you offer to do something, then remember to do it.

- Make it clear you don't expect your friend to return the favour, so they won't feel guilty for putting you out.

CHAPTER SEVEN

Will it ever get better?

It's now four years since Nick died, and five since the smiling consultant sat down on the edge of a hospital bed, called me 'Ma'am' and broke my heart.

I still mourn and I miss Nick deeply. He's often in my thoughts and his name is mentioned daily in our house by the girls, or me. We laugh when I tell them how much he hated custard at school dinners – it's Laura's favourite pudding – and they know how proud he would be of them as they grow and learn.

Yet the grief settles after a while. The first year is hard, with its enormous ups and downs. Great sweeping waves of emotion that take the breath right out of you, the tears that suddenly spring for no apparent reason. The time when a smell, a voice, an expression heard in passing will knock you for six because it was *him*. That fades, slowly but surely, and a heavy ache sets into its place. The raging grief settles into a sad acceptance that this awful thing really did happen and that it will never, ever change. Day by day you become accustomed to the idea that the person who made you complete will never walk back through the door and as you begin to grasp the reality of what this means you feel the weight of that knowledge settling in your stomach like a stone.

I can answer my girls' questions about their Dad now without crying. I can explain to a four year old how someone dies, what happens to their body, that yes they really did burn Daddy's body and that no, he didn't magically evaporate or rise from the green sofa through the ceiling to the clouds. I can tell people that my husband died and cope with the shock that flits across their faces before they gather their thoughts and try and say something appropriate. I can go to parties and talk about my children and be ready for the inevitable question, which doesn't always come but hangs, unspoken in the air.

Despite the passage of time I still mourn the loss of my soulmate. I miss my best friend. I ache to feel his big arms around my back, hear his laugh and that comforting, reassuring voice that made sure all was right with the world, even if things were going wrong.

His death has altered the course of my life. It has changed me, regardless of whether I marry again, have more children, have a dozen lovers or remain single. And part of the reason is that he is the man with whom I made my children and will always be their father. Even if I share my life with someone else, there will always be sadness that Nick isn't there to see his beautiful girls grow up and maybe have families of their own.

Where year one is the roller coaster, year two is the trench. You plough through it like knee deep mud until you come out the other end. There are fewer highs, and fewer desperate lows. People have seen you through the first year, you've done the first Christmas, you've had a birthday, his birthday has passed and finally you get to the magic anniversary. Nothing will be as bad as that first year, people say…

Oh no? The sad truth is that the second year, very often, is even harder. People drift away, go back to their own lives, get sick, have their own bereavements, get promoted, have babies, travel, move house, get divorced. Your story is shelved in the back of their minds. Occasionally they phone, but the cards and letters don't come on the special days and the year drags on relentlessly. You become more used to the new reality of your life, but the distance grows between you and the person you've lost.

And then it's year three. I, personally, found this even harder than year two though I know for many people it does begin to get better. A friend who had been bereaved for six years promised me it stopped going down after three and that you reach a level from where things begin to pick up. You get stronger, you cope better, you're more realistic… your expectations are lower.

Monika Key, a life coach and member of WAY, compares the journey through bereavement to the rings on a tree. "Every year a tree gets a new ring. Each ring represents circumstances during that year – some are good, some are hard. Every year we live and grow through our grief we get stronger."

We pass through survival mode, into an existence and then slowly but surely we begin to live again. But it takes time. It might be a year for some, it might be 10 for others.

Four years after Nick's death I do feel more positive about the future. I have begun to enjoy life rather than just exist and I know the importance of making the most of every single day. I'm amazed at how much I still miss him and mourn his loss for me and the children, and I know there will always be times when his death hits me just as hard as it did on day one and takes my breath away with the pain. Yet those days are now, thankfully, fewer and farther apart and I know that we have come through the worst.

So as a friend, relative, neighbour, colleague, what does all this mean? What should you expect? How can you cope with this long haul of grief?

People are unique, and bereaved people are too. Like anything else in life we each react to the situation in our own way, conditioned by who we are, what our life has been like and the nature of the situation we find ourselves in. No two deaths are the same and no two bereavements either. But there are some common threads that run through the experience for everyone:

- There is no set pattern to grief.

- You don't go through five well defined stages one after the other.

- You don't move steadfastly forward.

- You make progress, then you slip back, you have a few good days, then some terrible days. With time, the good days begin to outnumber the bad, but there will always be the odd bad day.

- You can't just 'snap out of' grief or 'pull yourself together'. You will heal in time, but you don't know how long it will take.

- You never know when the bad days are going to happen, or when the tears will come.

- You feel temporarily out of control of your life.

- You have to redefine who you are in relation to everyone you know.

- All your relationships will be affected – those with your children, parents, grandchildren, colleagues, neighbours and friends.

- You are not only grieving the death of the person you loved, but also the person you used to be and the life you shared. You're grieving for a future you had planned but will now never have.

One of the tricky things about bereavement is that it causes you to constantly look forward and back at the same time. You know you have to look forward, towards an unknown and uncertain future, but at the same time you can't help looking back to the past you shared with your loved one.

Your friends want you to look forward, to move on, but it is a necessary process to look back, to absorb, understand and deal with what has happened to you. Bit by bit the balance shifts and eventually you find yourself looking forward more than back, but there will always be momentary glances to where you've come from.

What can friends do, and how should you react?

- Be prepared for grief to last a long time. People don't suddenly 'get over this' in a year, or even two. Some mourn for the rest of their lives. There's no recipe or rule book, everyone is an individual. Rather than 'getting over' the death, your friend has to learn to absorb it and it will become part of who they are.

- Remember your friend has lost the person they were closest to, who was there day in, day out, keeping them company, encouraging them, supporting them and loving them. They've lost their best friend, their lover, the parent or grandparent of their children or grandchildren, possibly someone they've shared every day with for 30 or 40 years. They will need good friends now, more than ever and it will be a long, bumpy road. They may never be 'the same' again.

- Don't expect friends to behave as you think you would in similar circumstances. Accept the way they grieve – they're not you and they have their own feelings and ways of dealing with things.

- Don't tell them they have to 'get on with their life'. That's exactly what they are doing by simply getting up every day. Their life may not look quite how you think it should, or how it would if their husband or wife was still alive, but that's alright. After all, it's bound to be a very different life now.

- Talk about their husband or wife, and continue to do so over the years ahead. It is far more comforting to cry with a good friend than to have to pretend your partner never existed because they are never mentioned.

- Be patient. Your friend may be in shock, angry, scared and hurting. These feelings can last for months or years, certainly with less intensity over time, but they don't disappear magically after the first anniversary.

- If you ask a friend how they're feeling make sure you are prepared, and have time, to hear the answer.

- Don't tell them how to react, or behave, or that it's 'time to move on'. Don't judge.

- Remember your friend has changed as a person. She will never forget her husband, or his death. They will forever be part of who she is, the experience will have changed her, shaped her life and altered her outlook. It is impossible to be the same person she would otherwise have been.

- Keep in regular contact so you know how things really are. If you only phone every few months, your friend may well say he's been low even when there have been good times as well. He may fear that if he says he's fine you'll think 'Oh that's good, he's over it now, we can all go back to where we were'. You'll end up with a skewed view of how he's really doing.

- Continue to acknowledge special days – not necessarily the anniversary of the death, but perhaps a birthday, or wedding anniversary. Remember that friends will feel sad on their own birthday that their partner is not with them. Make an extra effort to remember their birthday.

- If you think you might have missed the anniversary and wanted to send a card, write anyway. Say you were thinking about them and knew it was a difficult time of year – that's enough and will be appreciated anyway, even if the card doesn't land on the mat on precisely the right day.

- Be positive. Encourage them. Tell them they're doing a good job. A bit of praise goes a long way and can really boost the spirits. Find out how they're really feeling and if they're low, listen to why they're hurting. Maybe all they need is a hug or some words of encouragement.

- Understand that it might be hard for your friend to hear about your life, especially if your lives were running along a similar path before his wife died. Now he's looking at you thinking this is where he would be if he wasn't widowed, and that can be painful. It might also go on for years and it's not his fault, so try not to blame him for it. Be sensitive about how you talk about your family, your wife, your husband, your holidays, your plans.

- Be careful how you talk about marital problems. It can be hard for someone who's lost a happy marriage through bereavement to hear friends complain about their own relationship. We all know relationships go through ups and downs, but it can be hard to hear that someone you care for may actually want to be without their partner when you'd give anything to be back with yours, warts and all.

- Don't try and tell your friend how he or she should be feeling. Their grief may well be uncomfortable for you to watch, but it's much harder for them to live with. Whatever they are feeling – sad, angry, bitter, depressed, sorry for themselves – is 'allowed' and acceptable. Those feelings are a natural response to what has happened. You may not think you'd react like that, and you may not, but you don't know, and it's unhelpful to project your own feelings onto a bereaved friend as the model for how they should behave.

- If your friend thinks you don't approve of the way they're grieving, they'll feel undermined at a time when they probably need reassurance, support and encouragement to keep going, rather than advice or instruction.

Finally, share their grief.

If your friend tells you he's missing his wife, try saying 'I miss her too'. It's so much more helpful than 'come on, she wouldn't want you to be miserable, there's a lot to live for'.

"Having someone to grieve with, three years in, is a Godsend. Most people, with all good intentions, want you to be over it by then. The fact is, you are never 'over it'; you just have to learn to live with it, and people are not doing you any favours by pretending that you are."

CHAPTER EIGHT

Buying the right gift

People often want to buy a gift for someone who's been bereaved. Flowers are the obvious choice, and a traditional gift. However think twice before you send a bouquet as soon as you hear your friend has been bereaved – there are other things that might be more appreciated. This may sound ungrateful but let me explain why:

- Flowers require space. If you've received three other bouquets already you won't have any space left.

- They require vases – you may have to buy new ones. You won't want to go shopping for vases two days after your partner has died.

- They can make the house smell like a funeral parlour, especially if they contain lilies, which most 'memorial' flowers do.

- They require fresh water and pollen can stain clothes, furniture and carpets – a nuisance that you really don't need at such a difficult time.

Alternatively, send something else straight after the death and then in a few months' time, send some flowers to say you were thinking of your friend – that is when they will be deeply appreciated and all the more so for being totally unexpected.

Here's a list of things that might go down much better with a newly bereaved friend:

- Alcohol (preferably good wine rather than a large bottle of vodka).

- Good food – see the chapter on food in this book for ideas.

- Chocolate or a favourite treat.

- Vouchers for a massage, reflexology session or other pampering treat to help your friend relax.

- Bubble bath.

- Your time. The promise of an evening/day/weekend spent together, or a firm commitment to look after children for a weekend is worth more than any other gift.

CHAPTER NINE

Just what do you say?

For many people the art of letter writing never happened, let alone died. Email and text messages have taken over as the main form of written communication and many younger people have never written a real letter by hand and posted it with a stamp.

But when someone you care about loses their partner, an email or text message simply isn't enough. It is one of the few times in life when you really have to put pen to paper and write a proper, old-fashioned letter.

Why?

Because the recipient can choose precisely when he or she reads it. She doesn't have to open it straight away and once she's read it, she can re-read it again and again.

There's no chance of it being deleted by mistake or lost forever when her computer crashes.

She can hold the letter physically in her hand – sounds odd but it can be very comforting.

Because you can put things in with the letter, for example photographs.

Because it can be kept for future generations.

Many bereaved people keep all the letters and cards they receive, tidied away in a box in the attic. Knowing they are there is a real comfort and there may be many times when they get the letters out and read them over, possibly even years later.

The letters will always be a reminder of how much their partner was loved and who by. They'll reinforce that the person was real and that he or she really did affect people's lives. They'll be a comfort to children who may learn new things about a parent who died young. They'll fill in the gaps of a life, giving the surviving partner clues to what other people felt and thought about their loved one, and will paint a picture of how that person was at work, with their friends, when they were younger.

Writing a condolence letter is undoubtedly hard, but it needn't be frightening and by sticking to a few guidelines anyone can do a good job of it.

GOLDEN RULES:

For simplicity's sake I'm imagining writing to a man whose wife has died:

- Write, don't phone. And if you're a close enough friend to phone, write a letter as well.

- If you don't write in the first week don't worry – write anyway.

- Try and write a letter, on plain writing paper. If you choose to send a card, blank is better than one that has a printed message such as 'thinking of you'. Such cards can look as if you didn't know what to say or didn't want to think about it.

- Don't try and be clever, or make it too long.

- Tell him you were saddened to hear about the death of his wife.

- Use her name – and never be afraid of saying it out loud to her husband.

- Tell him what she meant to you, and why. Tell him what a great friend she was, or how much fun, or how important she was to you or your children.

- Recount an anecdote of a happy or special time you spent together, if one stands out in your mind.

- Enclose a photograph if you have one that he might not have seen before.

- Don't promise anything you won't deliver. There's no point saying you'll always be there to help if you have no intention of doing it.

- Say you'll phone in a couple of weeks to see how he's getting on – and then do it.

- Don't ask him to phone you if he needs help – he won't be able to or want to.

- Don't tell him he'll be fine soon, or he'll get over it – he won't want to hear that now.

- Do tell him if you have been impressed by the way he dealt with her illness, or a sudden death, or how well he's looking after the children. Affirmation that you're doing well when you're feeling at your lowest ebb can be very comforting.

- Be careful what you say about God. Telling him it's what God wanted, or is God's will, is not helpful and you have no more idea of whether that is true than he does. These assumptions are not useful at such an early stage and may be totally inappropriate.

- Make sure you say clearly who you are – it can be hard to decipher signatures, especially ones with which you are unfamiliar.

If you didn't know them both

If you knew the person who died, but not the bereaved husband, tell him how you knew his wife and what she meant to your life. He may not immediately recognise a colleague's name, or that of someone from his children's school, especially if he is in shock. Yet letters from strangers can be enormously comforting because they help you realise your partner was treasured by more people than you knew.

If you know the surviving partner but didn't know his wife, perhaps he's a colleague at work, it's still important to write. Tell him you were aware of how much he loved his wife, that you know her death will be very hard for him and that you would like to support him in his grief. You can mention that you'd heard people speak highly of her, or that you'd been impressed by what he'd told you of her. Acknowledging his grief is just as important even if you can't say anything personal about your relationship with the person who has died.

A special gesture

Writing a condolence letter is a daunting task, particularly if you're not used to sending letters. But if you're not a natural letter writer then taking the trouble to do this will mean even more to your friend.

Remember, these letters don't have to be clever, or long. Simply putting one in the post is the most important part of the exercise – to show your friend you understand the enormity of what has happened, and are thinking about them.

For a week or two after bereavement letters and cards arrive almost every day and then, suddenly, the post stops coming and it's back to bills and brown envelopes. That can be a really tough moment when you're still feeling very fragile.

So don't panic if you don't send a letter on day one, and writing after the funeral has taken place is also fine. It's nice for the bereaved to hear that a funeral or memorial service was enjoyed and appreciated by friends and relatives.

For some people who have lost a partner, receiving condolence letters is just part and parcel of the whole experience but not something they relish. Letters can be a very blatant reminder of what has happened, and looking at cards sitting on a shelf can be difficult. Yet even for those who didn't enjoy receiving and reading the letters, the knowledge that many people loved and cared for their partner, and care enough about them to write, is valuable.

How people feel about condolence letters

"I found the letters of condolence, on the whole, to be a great comfort. I still get them out and read them… I keep thinking I should put them up in the loft, but when things are difficult, being reminded of what a special person Rob was really helps."

"The best ones share memories. Even things you didn't know, like her flatmate who said she was excited at meeting me but I didn't know. She was obviously playing hard to get..."

"The ones that spoke about Simon with love and kindness meant so much. I was also very moved by those letters that referred to the injustice of what had happened and the horror of it happening to our family. I felt and feel that so strongly, so for other people to articulate it was very supportive. I've kept all the letters and cards so that the children will be able to read them one day and know, if they didn't already, how greatly loved was their daddy."

"Ones that affirm you are encouraging. If it was a long illness, how you looked after them. How you complemented them or fulfilled them or whatever they observed."

"All the letters and cards were really valued by me but the personally written letters touched me far more than the cards. The cards with something written in touched me more than the ones with just a signature. Some expression of personal memory was hugely valued. I suppose it is the difference between 'I am sorry that someone you loved has died' and 'I am so sorry Mike has died, I will miss him and I have some understanding of your loss'."

"I was surprised at some of the letters I received because of who sent them and I was disappointed at others who didn't even bother. Because of the timing, my daily post was a mixture of Christmas cards and bereavement letters/cards. The unforgivable ones are those that combined both into one card!"

"The cards and letters that were personal, that took a moment to say something of how much Carol meant to the writer, will be those that are treasured longest. The ones that I really hated – and this may say

more about me than the writers – were those containing the platitudes like 'time heals'."

"A friend of mine wrote individual cards to the boys – not condolence cards, but just blank cards and in each of them she wrote of a memory of Steve specific to them – saying that it was something precious that could never be taken from them. What a lovely thing to do!"

"The condolence messages I really appreciated were those from people I'd never met. Because Steve's death was so high profile I had many from strangers. I particularly appreciated those where people had actually written more than their name."

"I remember the quantity – all those people who knew Rick and bothered to write. The ones that touched me most were from people that knew Rick but not me, especially if they did more than just sign the card."

"I was really touched by the one person who wrote to each of my children (then 15, 13 and eight). I haven't forgotten that and would certainly do that now in a similar circumstance, but probably wouldn't have thought of doing it before."

"Ones that acknowledge you and your heartache… Ones that make you cry. If you keep them and you need to cry, you can just bring them out and bring on the tears."

"I noticed that in a couple of cases, men who may have found it hard to verbalise what they were feeling about Rob's death, were able to express themselves in letters. The two I have in mind were from men who never talk on an emotional level, but wrote very profound things. eg 'Rob was the sort of minister I would love to have been but know I never could' and 'Rob was the most genuine caring person I have ever met.'"

"I like this one from France even if my translation is poor: 'S'il existait des mots qui puissent vous consoler, nous vous dirions du fond du coeur pour adoucir votre douleur.' (If there were words that could console you, we would say them from the bottom of our hearts to ease your pain.)"

"In some cases it is not about what they say. It is really appreciated if you hear from someone you wouldn't have expected to hear from, or receive anything from someone who was dropped from your Christmas card list years ago."

"It was just too soon after my wife's death to receive pre-printed cards with someone else's words on them, and I was so angry at the people who had sent them. I think it's the first thing they do really – hear the news, go to the card shop. Maybe I would have liked to have received hand written letters – they would have been more meaningful."

"Other helpful letters were the ones where specific help was offered, eg a cousin who lives a distance away near the sea, listed times when getting together might work, and offered us her house when they were away on holiday."

"Something that really upset me because I wasn't expecting it, was to get 'thinking of you' type cards on Rick's first birthday after he died, and on the first anniversary of his death. But worse somehow was the fact that there weren't any on the second, when I had geared myself up for them."

Appendix 1

Top things not to say to someone who's been widowed – and why

- I know how you feel.
  (*if you haven't been widowed you simply don't know how it feels*)

- At least he had a good innings.
  (*they spent the last 40 years together – the fact that he lived to 70 is little consolation to the widow who is now alone*)

- You're being so brave.
  (*she's not, she's just getting on with it*)

- Call me if you need anything.
  (*he won't be able to*)

- When my uncle died/when my Granny got cancer/when I got divorced etc.
  (*it's just not the same*)

- You have to move on/get over it/you should put your grief away.
  (*everyone grieves differently and it may take longer than you'd expect, he's not enjoying or revelling in his grief*)

- You should be resting, taking it easy, being kind to yourself.
  (*how? when you have a house to run, and maybe a living to earn and children to care for*)

The best things you can possibly say

- I'd like to do something to help – give me a job.

- I can only imagine how hard it is/how awful you feel.

- I miss him too.

- Spend Sunday with us, we'd love to have you.

- I remember when... tell stories about the person who has died.

- He'd be really proud of you.

- I'm going to take the children out for the whole day.

- You're doing a great job.

- Shall I come round and bring dinner with me?

- I'll do the driving.

- I'm so very sorry.

Appendix 2

Depression

It can be hard to know when a friend is depressed, rather than just feeling down. Experts say depression often manifests itself physically, rather than mentally, and because of this people often don't realise they are depressed. If you notice your friend is showing signs of five or more of the following symptoms, every day for over two weeks, then you should encourage them to seek help.

- feeling anxious, restless and/or agitated
- waking up early, having difficulty sleeping, having disturbing dreams
- feeling exhausted, having no energy
- loss of interest in food, losing or putting on weight
- persistently sad, crying a lot
- difficulty remembering things and/or concentrating
- complaining of physical aches and pains with no physical cause
- feeling irritable, angry, impatient more than usual
- being unable to get any pleasure out of things they usually enjoy

- loss of interest in sex

- feeling guilty

- loss of self-confidence and self-esteem

- feeling helpless or hopeless about the future, numb or empty

- avoiding other people, even close friends, not asking for support

- feeling scared of being left alone

- self-harming (by cutting themselves, for example)

- thinking about suicide

In its mildest form, depression won't stop someone leading a normal life, but will make everything harder to do and seem less worthwhile. At its most severe, clinical depression can be life threatening, because it can make people suicidal or simply give up the will to live.

It is important for people to be able to acknowledge and grieve over the death of someone close so that they can eventually move on with their life. Exploring and expressing feelings of grief means they are less likely to fester and contribute towards depression.

How can you help?

A depressed friend may well withdraw from you and other people, rather than ask for help or support. It is important to tell your friend that you are there to support them and are not going to abandon them. Stay in touch, and listen to what they are saying when you do speak to each other. Show that you care by listening and being affectionate and by spending time with them. Praise their achievements to increase their confidence and help them feel good about themselves, and encourage them to help themselves in small ways – by joining a support group, doing some relaxation classes such as yoga or similar, getting some exercise or eating healthy food. All of these will lift their mood and help break the cycle of negative thoughts that can feed on themselves. Finding a suitable support group for them is a helpful thing to do – see the White Ladder website for details of bereavement support groups (**www.whiteladderpress.com**).

Whatever you do, don't tell them to stop feeling sorry for themselves, or that there's always someone worse off than they are. Try not to blame them for being depressed, or tell them to 'pull themselves together'. Praise is much more effective than criticism, which can lead to them becoming more depressed. You can reassure a friend that they can do things to improve their situation, but you have to do this in a caring and sympathetic way.

Contact us

You're welcome to contact White Ladder Press if you have any questions or comments for either us or the authors. Please use whichever of the following routes suits you.

Phone: 01803 813343

Email: enquiries@whiteladderpress.com

Fax: 01803 813928

Address: White Ladder Press, Great Ambrook, Near Ipplepen, Devon TQ12 5UL

Website: www.whiteladderpress.com

What can our website do for you?

If you want more information about any of our books, you'll find it at **www.whiteladderpress.com**. In particular you'll find extracts from each of our books, and reviews of those that are already published. We also run special offers on future titles if you order online before publication. And you can request a copy of our free catalogue.

Many of our books have links pages, useful addresses and so on relevant to the subject of the book. You'll also find out a bit more about us and, if you're a writer yourself, you'll find our submission guidelines for authors. So please check us out and let us know if you have any comments, questions or suggestions.

Fancy another good read?

If you've found **If There's Anything I Can Do...** helpful, how about trying another of our books? Very often it's the death of one parent that sets the other off on a downward decline that you struggle to help them through. It's a deeply traumatic moment when you realise that, having depended on your parents all your life, suddenly they are dependent on you.

Rosie Staal's thoughtful and practical book **What Shall We Do With Mother?** follows the stories of several people who have struggled at times to help an ageing parent. According to Claire Rayner, "The book manages to be three things all at the same time, which is very remarkable. It is readable, humorous and extremely informative."

Here's a taster of what you'll find in **What Shall We Do With Mother?** If you think it would be helpful and want to order a copy, you can call us on 01803 813343 or order online at **www.whiteladderpress.com**.

Extract from *What Shall We Do With Mother?*

Anthea's story

When Anthea's husband died she was poleaxed. He'd always done everything round the house, made all the decisions and just about done her thinking for her. Left alone, she seemed hardly capable of breathing unaided. Bob, her son, despaired. "Her GP told me she'd need a lot of careful handling, plenty of attention and probably some counselling. We gave her the lot, and more, but she barely responded.

"It was awful to see her decline so badly, but she just didn't seem to want to live. Nothing we did made any difference. It was as though she was shrivelling up into a little ball waiting to die.

"Of course we felt sorry for her, but at the same time we feared for her sanity – and for our own. We also couldn't bear to think about the future. We just pinned our hopes on a softly-softly approach and a gradual turning round, away from bleakness into some kind of normality."

Bob and his sister, Kate, say they felt so guilty about not being able to be with her as much as they felt she needed them that they started telephoning every day, one of them at lunchtime, the other in the early evening. It soon became a dreadful chore, punctuating their busy lives, but they knew that once they'd got into the routine there was no easy way out. Stopping the phone calls, or even reducing them, would, they were sure, increase Anthea's insecurity because she often told them how much she enjoyed the daily chats.

Anthea's house had been on the market at the time of her husband's death. Their plan had been to move out of rural Hertfordshire and nearer Bob and Kate and their families in London. Against her Ofcaps' advice, the new widow went ahead with the sale of the house which had so many happy memories. But then, instead of making the planned move, she decided to stay in the same village, choosing to buy a thatched cottage with four bedrooms and an unnecessarily large garden.

"It was a case of out of the frying pan and into the fire," Bob says. "Nothing would deflect her from this completely insane, irrational step. And, of course, as soon as she had made the move, she regretted it.

"She used to say she could hear Dad talking to her in the old house, but there was just an echoing silence in the new one. It was the worst thing she could ever have done."

Faced with such intractability in their Mother, Bob and Kate did all they possibly could to influence her into making what they could see was the right decision. They failed. She would not listen and went her own way. In a situation like this, you can only give your best advice – and, of course, resist the temptation later to say 'I told you so'.

Anthea's distress manifested itself in a number of ways, most notably in a withdrawal into a deep trough of depression. Her apathy even extended to her grandchildren in whom she now showed little interest, visiting them only once in London – and that was because protocol demanded she attend the christening of the new baby.

"There's no reason for me to go on living," she would say flatly to anyone brave enough to ask her how she was getting on.

Bob reckons it was hard to argue with her on that fact, despite the valiant efforts he and his sister made for more than two years. "We tried to involve her in our lives as much as possible," he says, "but she made it clear we were wasting our time. She alienated most of her friends, and those who remained in touch did so only through a sense of duty.

"It was tragic. She would just sit staring at photographs of Dad most of the time. The whole house was full of them so he was all around her.

"My sister and I arranged for Mum to have counselling when we realised she wasn't making any progress. It made a difference, if only because it enabled Mum to moan 'officially', but after about 18 months I think the poor counsellor was on the verge of a nervous breakdown. We could hardly blame her."

The biggest stumbling block in trying to help with counselling is attitude. Older people do not respond happily to the idea of sharing innermost thoughts or intimate details with someone else – whether that someone is a close family member or a complete stranger.

Some Age Concern branches offer counselling as one of their services, but it tends not to be readily seized upon as a useful lifeline by those who could most benefit from it. "It's very much an attitude of their age – they're just not comfortable with the idea," a voluntary trained counsellor says. "They don't open up, so they keep their troubles to themselves. It's a shame, because counselling can definitely help."

Distraction can be therapeutic, too, so try and encourage a troubled, grieving Mum to make a scrapbook of her memories. Assure her that the whole family would like it, as a source of interest and pleasure, but also as a tribute to Dad. Levels of motivation will be at zero, so don't expect her to whip out the scissors and glue and create something worthy of a Blue Peter badge all on her own. Do it with her, then you both get all sorts of benefits, not least the pleasure of each other's company.

As an incentive, keep focused on the best spin-off you could hope for: that Mum will become so heartily sick of dwelling on the past that she'll get to the end of the scrapbook project as quickly as possible, lock it away in a cupboard, and start looking the world in the face again.